# Every Monday

## Finding God on Tough Days

### Craig H. Smith

authorHOUSE®

*AuthorHouse™*
*1663 Liberty Drive, Suite 200*
*Bloomington, IN 47403*
*www.authorhouse.com*
*Phone: 1-800-839-8640*

*First published by AuthorHouse 4/23/2009*

*ISBN: 978-1-4389-3922-3 (sc)*
*ISBN: 978-1-4389-3923-0 (hc)*


*Library of Congress Control Number: 2009900173*

*Printed in the United States of America*
*Bloomington, Indiana*

*This book is printed on acid-free paper.*

# *Dedication*

The enterprise of writing a book has been a monumental adventure for me. The journey began with God's unlikely call on my life. This call to church leadership never ceases to amaze me. Even today, as I pen these words, I am taken aback by my Creator's persistent nudge into leadership roles. Praise be to God for His truly remarkable grace and incredible capacity to use ordinary vessels to perform Kingdom work.

I dedicate this book to each one of the *everyday* church leaders who dared to respond to God's call to depart safety-zone living and venture into the uncharted territory of leadership. In so doing, you make Kingdom-impact in the lives of the persons and the institutions around you. Your quiet loyalty, unheralded devotion, and unwavering strength are the epicenter of a great heaven-quake whose soundless tremor of positive force ripples across time and shakes the world. Thank you!

To Victoria, my wife, lover, and best friend: You are my motivation and unfailing support. You believed in me long before I believed in myself. It is largely through your encouragement, confidence, and faith that this book is even possible. You are indeed a *Proverbs-Thirty-One Woman* and the love of my life. I adore you! Thank you so very much.

To my family: I cannot imagine ministry without genuine love and wholehearted support of family. Mark & Kimberly: Gracie, Dakoda, Topher, & Abigail; Jason & Steffanie: Samantha, Sarah, & Keri; Brian & Nicole: Isabel, Ian, & Evan; Kenneth & Tanya: Lily, Elijah, & Chloe. You enrich my life and keep me real. Thanks for blessing me.

To my readers: May God bless you, encourage you, and challenge you through the words and stories that follow. May some word, some phrase, or some story in these pages enlarge your love for the Savior, embolden your call to ministry, and give you confidence to live life large.

Keep learning. Keep loving. Keep leading!

# *Acknowledgements*

With any significant enterprise, the final product is a team effort. This book is no exception. I want to express my personal and sincerest thanks to:

Ina Rae Longwell – without your expertise and willingness to come along side me, this project could have simply remained a daydream. Thanks for encouraging me with your time, talent, and generous spirit.

George Gallup, Jr. – your graciousness and enthusiastic willingness to hang in there with a first-timer is remarkable. Your deep faith commitment is an inspiration. You have blessed me.

Marlene Bagnull – your writer's conference, practical advise, early affirmations, and draft editing helped to set the sails. Much thanks.

Victoria J. Smith – you believe in me. What stronger foundation can there be? You are my love and partner in all of life's adventures.

Church of the Brethren community – your congregations, colleagues, institutions, and agencies have provided me with a leadership laboratory.

AuthorHouse Publishing – you open the door for new voices to be heard.

# Foreword

"Blue Mondays" are a common occurrence, with most people who experience these "down days" content to wait them out. Craig Smith, however, sees these periods as offering a valuable opportunity to gain new spiritual insights and to grow in faith. It is said that God often speaks most profoundly to us when we are tired and discouraged.

*Every Monday* is a devotional book directed especially to Christian leaders, clergy, youth leaders, church staff members, missionaries, and others. Few groups experience a greater Monday "let-down" than church leaders after the Sunday "high" of religious celebration. The American people, surveys show, feel that the role of clergy is one of the most difficult and challenging of all the professions.

In his book, Smith offers readers forty brief stories about his own personal experiences and encounters that have brought home to him some powerful spiritual message and have challenged him in new ways. These messages include fresh visions for leadership; reminders of the need to look beneath the surface of life; encouragement to plunge boldly and faithfully into unfamiliar territory; and an emphasis on the importance of staying in step with the Lord, regardless of one's present mood and circumstances.

Craig Smith's stories or vignettes cover a wide range of settings, from the somber visit to the site of the Twin Towers in New York City, to lighter venues such as dancing, clothes, football, fast food, driving, and the wonders of nature. The author tells his stories in a lively manner, often injecting humor, and drawing upon his own broad and deep experience, gained in 30 years of ministry as a pastor, teacher, counselor, coach, and businessman.

The author concludes each of his stories with a powerful and memorable prayer that incorporates the spiritual insights he has gained from this story.

Craig Smith's book should find its place at the bedside, breakfast table, or desk of every Christian leader, to be read not only on Mondays, but also on other days as well.

*Every Monday* will not only lift·readers out of their doldrums, but also encourage them to sharpen their own observational skills, as they see the hidden power . . . the hand of the Lord . . . in the common scene. In story after story Craig Smith underscores the fact that "we are never alone."

George Gallup, Jr.
Founding Chairman
The George H. Gallup International Institute

# Table of Contents

# Confessions of a Fleeing Leader

I ran away from God for a long, long time. Frankly, I was pretty good at it. Oh, I knew *about* God. My grandmother took me to church. I attended MYF (Methodist Youth Fellowship). I participated in Vacation Bible School. I even had my fair share of warm fuzzy God-feelings at Epworth Forest Church Camp, but I managed to keep God's call at a safe distance.

With minor wear and tear on my small-town psyche, I survived being a chubby little kid. My parents were good people. They both worked outside the home yet managed to provide most everything that an only child could want. My grandmother, who lived with us, died when I was twelve. Henry, my dog and constant companion, was "put to sleep" the day before I left for college. Nevertheless, for the most part, I did okay.

Along the path of boyhood, I learned to love sports and even won my fair share of awards. I discovered girls at an early age and engineered a healthy dating plan. I even owned a couple of cars, including a 1957 Studebaker station wagon that the gang (a good term in those days) nicknamed *The Blue Eagle*.

Manchester College brought studies, a few more dates (the best ones were with Victoria Jean Sayers), and more sports. I had it—my life—all planned out. I was destined to be a great college football coach except for one thing; in the last semester of my senior year of college, I discovered that I hated teaching! Here is the sequence that followed: Considerable oops! Plan change. Life shift. Vocational nomadic phase. Eventual segue into business.

Business life was favorable for a season. I married Victoria and we had our first three little girls. We owned a charming house on a full acre of land in a nice suburb of Columbus, Ohio. A small creek meandered through the back of the property. Every now and then I would go to that creek, listen to the water trickle over the rocks, think about life, and wonder about God. Our family even joined a local United Methodist church just down the road. Life was good. Well, almost.

I could easily ramble on about this personal life stuff. But my point is this: I persisted in running away from God and his call on my life—his call to make me his own. When I finally stopped running and succumbed to Christ's tolerant beckoning, he filled an enormously empty chasm in the core of my soul. Yet somehow, I knew there was more. Jesus was calling me to do something more than just believe in him. He was calling me to more than an intellectual grasp of the facts about his existence; it was something more than an emotional assent to lofty feelings about God. He was calling me to know him, love him, commit to him, and ultimately serve him.

I was scared to death! I was fairly certain that Jesus had simply confused me with some other much more talented person who just happened to have the same name! Obviously, this was a simple mistake in ministerial and leadership identity.

After many clarifying moments alone with the Lord, I told him that I would do whatever he wanted me to do and go wherever he wanted me to go, just as long as he didn't put me in a church! After all, I didn't like to get up in front of people. I wasn't a good reader, especially in public (a fear from childhood); and I didn't know how to act like a pastor. While I was pretty certain that God knew most of this stuff, I needed to be sure. So, I told him.

One long and sleepless night, I tossed and turned and finally blurted out, "Okay! Okay, Lord. I'll do it. I'll do whatever you want me to do. I'll go wherever you want me to go . . . (long pause) even a church." Immediately, I sensed a gigantic crane hover over me, lower a winch, and hoist an incredible invisible weight off my chest. At that moment, an unforgettable quiet came to rest right where the unbearable weight had lodged. This quiet filled me with immeasurable peace, and nothing has ever been the same.

So, what about you? Have you ever tried to run from God? Any fleeing church leaders among you? Any reluctant prophets?

Stammering preachers? Hesitant deacons? If so, it's okay. Because here is the important thing: when you allow your story to meet God's story, there is always a better story to tell.

## *The Leader's Prayer:*

Pursuing God . . . you are faster than my flight. You are stronger than my fear. Your sweet persistent hunt for my life leaves me in awe. Thank you for seeing gifts within me when I could not see them in myself. By your enduring grace show me how to keep investing these gifts in your Kingdom's work. In the name of the One who sees very unique traits in very common places . . . Amen.

# Dancing Grapes

At one of our regional church conferences, the judicatory leadership chose a theme from John 15. In this chapter Jesus told an amazing story by painting word images to describe the landscape and operation of a vineyard. His intention was to explore the model of a true believer's life and his relationship to the divine.

Jesus unashamedly broadcast the nature and identity of the vine, the branches, the labor, the process, the life-flow, the necessary connectedness, the desired growth, and the sweet sweet fruit of a life directly connected to him! The bottom line of the story . . . the bottom line of the vineyard . . . the bottom line of the process . . . and the bottom line of the labor is this: there is a divine plan for all ages. Every true believer and disciple of Jesus Christ is to "abide" in him, bear much fruit, and experience the overflow with his joy!

How fitting it would be for us, as members of Christ's body, to recommit ourselves to a radical connectedness with the True Vine. How phenomenal it would be for the branches to embrace the pruning of the Vinedresser. How mind-blowing if the branches would dare to call out to the Vinedresser, "Come and take care of us. Hurry! We need you! We need your attention. We need you to prune away *everything* that impedes our fruit-bearing growth for you. Cut away our constant complaining about non-essential issues. Sever our persistent outcries for *my way* in music and worship styles. Lop off the *me-and-my-church* mentality that restricts your creative life-flow within us. Bring down strongholds of a religious spirit and in-fill us with discernment, power, and the compassion of your Holy Spirit. Trim back the bureaucracy of our church life and refresh us in the cool running streams of authentic ministry. Sheer away our haughty self-reliant strategies and reconnect us to the One who is our True Vine."

My spirit cries out, "Take me to that place! Take me to the place where the branches are deeply engrafted into the Vine, where the soil is rich with provision, the leaves blow freely in the breeze, and the grapes dance with joyful anticipation. Yes, take me to the vineyard that is filled with a bumper crop of mouth-watering fruit, where the sun shines brightly, where the land is rich, where the water flows freely, and where the Vinedresser smiles." What a festive chateau that would be!

Along the way, however, there are noteworthy specifics to keep in mind. If we are to take this journey and arrive at this notable, worthy estate, church leaders must remember these:

1. Sour grapes create too much *whine.*

2. Pruning is crucial for growth.

3. Sweet, long-lasting fruit is produced exclusively through The Vine.

4. Forever and a day, the harvest must be washed and stored in prayer, praise, and worship.

5. The finished product ought to be dispensed in preaching, teaching, and compassionate acts of service.

6. Always use God-honoring vessels.

7. Grapes grow in the vineyard but most of the wine is sent out.

8. Primary connectedness is to the Vine not to the cluster.

While I am fairly certain that grapes do not actually dance, I am equally certain that Jesus' vineyard is a place to celebrate our uncompromising relationship and connection to him. And in the process, if a Chardonnay should happen to tango with a Merlot, so be it!

## *The Leader's Prayer:*

Lord of the Vineyard and of the Dance . . . fill my cup! May I drink the new wine of your Spirit and be set free to dance to a new song. Keep me connected to the Vine of Real Life. Pour yourself out into the chalice of each day that I might taste and see that you are <u>still</u> good. In the name of Jesus, the True Vine . . . Amen.

# The Juggling Act

How many balls can you keep in the air at the same time? What about plates? Can you spin them? Okay, how many? Three, four, nine, twelve? Can you do hoops or rings or clubs? How about flaming batons—the kind with fire blazing from both ends?

Is it just me, or does ministry ever feel like a juggling act? If it's just me, stop reading; you are just wasting your time. If, however, you ever feel like your life and ministry are spinning out of control, read on.

Ministry, whether it's my job as a church executive, or your job as a heavily involved lay person or pastor of a church, is by some weird definition a juggling act. Once you heave the small red meeting ball into the air, here comes the counseling plate. Catch the ball and spin the plate. With these in motion, you grab the funeral hoop and the wedding ring and the flaming crisis baton. Keep it moving! Get it up there! Higher! Move it! Move it! Move it! Launch the newsletter, fit in the phone, fling the files, boost the Bible study, pitch the Junior-High-camp-out tent, let the sermon fly, rotate a retreat, loft the purpose statement, and, don't forget to toss in a visit to Aunt Mabel at the *Shady Rest Nursing Home For Prominent Members*. Oh yea, one more thing—remember to relax and take some time for yourself and your family!

I know where church leaders live. It's not really Cirque du Soleil, but I recognize that it can feel that way some days—even some weeks, some months, or some years. For that reason, you are invited to come to the show, step under the *Big Top in the Sky*, and listen to the Ring Master. Wearing his traditional red suit and black top hat, he strides to the middle of the performance arena, takes his prominent place at center stage, and asks the grand *Ministry Question of the Day*. "Ladies and gentlemen of ministry, boys and girls of help and hope: how in the world do you juggle all of this incredible stuff and not get buried in a high wire, aerial collapse?"

The church leaders gathered in the bleachers look on with silent understanding. They know that they can perform this astounding trick for awhile. They know that they can juggle an incredible amount of work. But they also know that far too often things cave in—crash and burn; tumble to the ground; plummet to death—all around them.

With all of this in mind, let me suggest that *what you hold on to* is far more important than *what you keep in the air*. When Jesus was teaching about establishing a pattern for would-be-life-jugglers, he told them, "apart from me you can do *nothing*" (reference, italics mine). Jesus seems to be saying that—without his abiding presence, his sustaining power, and his ongoing coaching— jugglers can't even toss a single ball or spin a solitary plate! That means us—well intentioned, well trained, and exceedingly dedicated Christian leaders—can do *nothing*!

Consequently, when you are juggling your schedule, balancing your *Blackberry*, downloading your *Outlook*, rolling your eyes, spinning your head, launching your new venture, and on the verge of tossing it all in, try holding on to these:

- Hold his Word in your mind.

- Hold his authority in your labor.

- Hold his humility in your example.

- Hold his song in your heart.

- Hold his love in your approach.

With these held tightly, go juggle, spin, toss, preach, teach, visit, and serve, knowing that the One whom you hold is ultimately the One who is holding you.

## *The Leader's Prayer:*

God who spins the earth, tosses the waves, and holds the stars in space . . . strengthen my grip and my focus. Help me to understand that more is not better, that faster is not sacred, and that fatigue is not holy. In this *Juggling Act of Ministry*, join me each day to the One without whom I can do absolutely *nothing*. In his unparalleled name . . . Amen.

# Ground Zero

Devastation grabs my heart. Stench fills my nostrils. Silence breaks with weeping. Bewilderment joins anger and sadness as orders of the day. Words get in the way and emerge only as an incredibly pitiful surrogate for birthing the raw images and emotions of the scene at Ground Zero.

Within a few short weeks of the heartrending events known as 9/11, I was invited to speak at a Thanksgiving Memorial Service in Brooklyn, New York. The Sunday Morning Service was planned to honor the heroic members of a New York City Fire Department Ladder Company. At my wife's urging and filled with a holy dash of chutzpah, I asked the local pastor if it was feasible to venture into Manhattan and get a closer look at Ground Zero. Little did I realize that God would use this somewhat bold request to take us deep into the core of the devastation.

Brother Edwin (Eddie) Quijano, a retired NYPD detective and member of the church, met us in Brooklyn and graciously guided us through the subway system into south Manhattan. As we climbed the steps to street level and turned the corner onto a short side street, Eddie said, "There it is." Several blocks in the distance the smoldering ruins of the Twin Towers popped into view. The scene hung there, framed like a deep black hole in the Manhattan skyline.

"Do you want to go closer?" Eddie quizzed.

"Yes!" blurted my wife with a swift yet uncomfortable reply.

We moved closer. The ominous destruction of this horrible act loomed ever more real. Eddie paused to chat with a couple of his former NYPD colleagues. After introducing us and explaining we had traveled to the city for me to preach at the Memorial Service, a captain asked if we wanted to "go in." We agreed and were promptly ushered behind the police barricade. In short order a Police Community Service van arrived to escort us to the perimeter of Ground Zero. Following a brief tour of the interior periphery, the Community Service Officer questioned Eddie if he and his guests would like to "go farther." An affirming nod ushered us closer to the core.

National-Guard-Security-Team clearance was secured and we waited for our turn. In those moments we respectfully watched family members shepherded into the huge common grave that swallowed up their loved ones. With hard hats on their heads, tears streaming down their cheeks, teddy bears clasped to their chests, and flowers clutched in their hands, grieving family members filed in. Minutes later, like a casket-less funeral procession, husbands and wives, moms and dads, brothers and sisters, grandmothers and grandfathers, and aunts and uncles simply filed out—a joyless march from an unthinkable tomb to a grief-laden home filled with a countless string of empty tomorrows.

At last, it was our turn. We walked directly to the platform—the place erected for President Bush and Mayor Giuliani. Time halted. An eerie miasma lingered. Speechless, we gazed into the stinking, steaming pit of rubble which just weeks before had graced Manhattan's skyline as a symbol of New York City's global grandeur, architectural splendor, world-wide prestige, and international financial prowess. Now this icon of achievement had been reduced to piles of hellish smoldering debris, chunks of strewn concrete, twisted configurations of steel, tons of shattered glass, shrouds of orange safety mesh, and the ashes of cremated human flesh. We gawped. We cried. We prayed. We left.

Sometimes leadership takes us on journeys we would not choose. Sometimes leadership takes us to places we do not wish to see. But on that Sunday morning, as I looked into the eyes of those courageous New York City firefighters, I knew that this journey to Ground Zero had taken all of us to a strange new place deep inside. They had been there. I had been there. And, God . . . well, in spite of it all, he was *still* there.

## The Leader's Prayer:

God of Strange Journeys . . . bear with me, be with me, and put up with me and my reluctance to travel to difficult places. When all around seems to speed out of control, rally to my aid. Confirm your compassion, your attention, your sovereign rule. When deeds and circumstances make no sense, be my rock, my fortress, my repose. Furnish me with the words—or the suitable silence—to mirror your certain presence. Help me to look into the eyes of those who need to see you and to fulfill their longing. In the name of the One whose eyes are clearly on you . . . Amen.

# Vignettes

Martha Stewart is out of jail and back on the air. A high profile Hollywood celebrity is filing for divorce, and before the ink is dry, a new engagement is announced . . . again! Another superstar is found innocent . . . or at least found not guilty. George Steinbrenner is spending $880 million of his own money to build a new Yankee Stadium. A gorgeous deep blue jeweled Versace gown was worn to a recent charity fundraising extravaganza by yet another young starlet. Millions of dollars are made by the latest, must-see films hitting the big screen for the seasonal blockbuster blitz. And Kathy Lee Gifford has finally found significant work since leaving Regis. So, do you feel better knowing all of this? Does it make your life any better?

While our nation is fascinated with pop culture news, the real world moves on. For many of us, our *real world* is the church.

Given the tsunami-like waves of pop culture and our trickling brook of church culture, church life can often seem insignificant, mundane, or downright boring! When is the last time the church rolled out a *Red Carpet* for its leaders to walk down before delivering a Committee Report to the semi-annual Congregational Business Meeting? How often have you been chased by a wild band of pious paparazzi as you left your home to drive off to a Church Board Meeting? How many reporters are camped outside your door poised to capture your next utterance in worldwide print? How many invitations are you getting from your agent to be the next international spokesperson for Calvin Klein, BMW, Nike, Starbucks, Verizon, Nintendo's Wii, or The Gap?

As this American enlightenment carries on its exciting love affair with pop culture, our seemingly pathetic ministry life appears to drone on. Yet, there are those moments, there are those times, there are those occasions, when the real world of ministry comes alive and shines brighter than we might ever imagine. There are those vignettes of grace and hope and peace and understanding–moments of indescribable delight–that burst into our *every-day-same-ole-same-ole-life* and make the church humdrum glisten and glow and shimmer and frolic with pure joy.

No major news network, not even CNN or FOX, will break into broadcasting to report these headlines:

*Jackie Makes a Decision for Jesus*

*Jones Family Comes Through Tough Time, Marriage Survives*

*Camp Counselor Shares Divine Love — Abused Child Brought to Safety*

*Today's Sermon Breaks Down Wall — Karen Smith Freed From Anger and Bitterness*

*Pastor Sue's Prayer Delivers Ton of Peace*

*Quiet Time Alone with God Changes Jeff Milligan's Heart*

*Deacon's Visit Turns Tide on Lonely Day*

These news flashes will never interrupt regular programming or scroll across the bottom of a broadcast screen. The pop culture will never even notice. There will be no Red Carpet, no reporters, no paparazzi, and no endorsements. But I can assure you of this: there is Someone who notices. There is Someone who takes in every word of these seemingly buried stories. There is Someone who turns water into wine, fig trees into lessons, and sand into redeeming messages of hope; and he takes the mundane tasks of ministry and turns them into vignettes of eternal delight.

## The Leader's Prayer:

Dear Friend of Leaders . . . the world knew you not. Culture was not impressed when you were ushered from your mother's womb. Some noticed, but most of the world simply went on its merry (or miserable) way. But, *You* are the headline of the ages, the Bright Morning Star, the King of Kings, the Lord of Lords, and the Christ! You are the Father's ultimate Vignette of Grace, and you are my eternal delight. In the midst of the mundane, show me the hidden plot, the buried headlines, the Good News behind the good news. In this way I will learn to look for your headlines—the ones that *really* matter. In the name of the One whose name fills the front page of heaven . . . Amen.

# Hiding Places

Do you have any good hiding places? This is neither a question from one of my grandchildren ready to embark on a winner-take-all game of *Hide and Seek,* nor have I been engaged by the Secret Service to discover innovative undisclosed locations for former Vice-Presidents to hang out in times of national crisis. *Do you have any good hiding places* is primarily a question about the dynamics of leadership. If truth be told, it must be said that we all need a good hiding place every now and then.

So, where do you hide? When there are repeated blasts of hot air from the fiery furnace of criticism; when somebody leaves a verbal dagger in your back; when Sister Sue says she has been neglected in the weekly distribution of your attention; when Deacon Dave notes the shallow nature of your new fangled preaching; when the thick, juicy quicksand of victimizing gossip seems to give way under your feet and sucks you under; when you are bone-weary from church politics . . . where do you go to retreat, to escape, to hide?

In my younger days of ministry, I used to pretend that I didn't need to hide. I was strong. I was spiritual. I was capable. I was a Christian, a pastor, an example, a church leader of the highest order! I know this sounds pretty regal, but leaders are supposed to "buck up" and be strong. Right? After all, hiding places are for the scared, the weak, the fragile, the anemic—spiritual sissies of the highest order. I didn't want to be one of *those*! Nevertheless, time, age, and circumstances—a trinity of reality checks—have proven me wrong. Sometimes I am scared; I am weak; I am fragile; I am spiritually anemic and a sissy of the uppermost faith order. I may not want to be one of *those*, but I am. So sometimes, in my weakness and imperfection, I hide.

Occasionally, I hide in the car. Now and then I will just get in the car and drive—no iPod, no radio, no leadership-learning CD, no human conversation. I just drive; and somewhere along the way, I begin to have a chat with God. He listens. I sit in silence and wait. God speaks. I listen. Once in a while, overcome by his presence and grace, tears stream down my face. There have been times when I didn't really want to arrive at my destination; I wanted to keep driving, keep hiding, and keep safe in his presence.

Often, I hide in the Scriptures. I especially like to hide in the Psalms. One of my favorite hiding places is Psalm 62. Listen [italics represent my interpretive slant]:

For God alone my soul waits in silence;

from him comes my salvation.

He only is my rock and my salvation,

*my high-walled shelter of protection*;

I shall not be greatly moved.

For God alone my soul waits in silence,

for my hope is from him.

He only is my rock and my salvation,

*my city of safety;* I shall not be shaken.

On God rests my deliverance and my honor;

my mighty rock, *my can't-nobody-hurt-me-here place* is God.

Trust in him at all times—*especially when you need to hide*—O people; pour out your heart before him;

God is a refuge—*a place to hide and to seek, a place to sense the Highest Security*—for us. (verses 1-2, 5-8 RSV).

As a Christian leader, being hurt is not an option. It is a reality. It is not a matter of "if" hurt happens but "when" hurt happens. Spiritual injury comes with the territory. So, my recommendation for leaders is to find a hiding place for your soul and to visit as often as needed.

## The Leader's Prayer:

God of Safety and Refuge . . . thank you for being there. Thank you for listening. Thank you for caring. Thank you for never tiring of my visits. Thank you for being my rock, my fortress, my deliverance, my honor, my hope. You are my hiding place, my counselor, and the still small voice who speaks peace into my anxious spirit; healing into my wounded soul; and focused strength into my fragile leadership. In the name of Jesus, the One who often slipped away to gardens, mountainsides, and out-of-the-way places to simply take sanctuary in you . . . Amen.

# Bad Spellers . . . Untie!

Iwear mono-vision contacts. My left contact is for seeing close-up—reading, paperwork, computer tasks—the things right in front of me. My right contact is for distance—driving, seeing my wife across the kitchen table in the morning, watching the Super Bowl—the things that are more than eighteen inches away!

Years ago, when I first began to wear these lenses, I was told by my doctor that "Even though these two lenses seem to be working against each other, your brain will figure it all out and adjust." So, I tried it. And guess what? Dr. Laura was right! My brain did exactly that. My amazing gray matter sifted through all of the calculations, made all of the fine adjustments, and (voila!) I can see!

I've always thought that this brain-adjustment-thing was pretty neat. Recently, however, I was introduced to a whole new theory in this area. This new concept takes my appreciation and understanding of *brain adjustment* to a whole new level. The brain really can do some amazing things.

Just for the fun of it, try this. Here are the instructions. Read all of the following sentences straight through without *over-thinking* them.

Acocdrnig to an elgnsih unviesitry sutdy, the oredr of letetrs in a wrod dosen't mttaer. The olny iopmrantt thnig is that the frsit and lsat ltteer of eevry word is in the crcreot ptoision. The rset can be jmbueld and one is stlil able to raed the txet wiohtut dclftfuiiy. Tihs is bcuseae the huamn mnid deos not raed ervey lteter by istlef, but the wrod as a wlohe. (Adapted from *The Significance of Letter Position in Word Recognition*, a 1976 Nottingham University Ph. D. thesis by Graham Rawlinson. Text first circulated on the internet in September 2003.)

Wow! Is that cool or what! I am so fascinated with this new jumblese that I've already begun to establish useable applications. Here are just a cpuole. No more sepll chcek. What a tmie saver. I'm a bad speller, but so what. Bad spellres of the wrold untie!

I can finally relax and let my brain figure it all out. Think about it. There will be fewer ridiculous bulletin bloopers, less agonizing over agenda lapses, and sermon notes and board minutes would never need to be edited. We could finally live pecaefluly, smiply, tgoehter.

Now, as a leader in the church, consider this. Jesus *is* our Alpha and Omega—the Beginning and the End, the First and the Last, the Author and Finisher of our faith. So, if the Alpha and Omega—the Beginning and the End, the First and the Last, the Author and Finisher of our faith—is in the proper place, everything else works itself out. If we as leaders can get this right—if we can simply get Jesus in the right place—then whatever happens in-between (as confusing, jumbled, or mixed-up as it might seem) doesn't really matter as much. We can somehow persist with grace, confidence, and the calm assurance that we can still see God's Big Picture.

### *The Leader's Prayer:*

Lord of the In-Between . . . I confess to you that I don't always get it right. I often get this ministry thing all jumbled up. I know that you are the Alpha and the Omega—the Beginning and the End. But sometimes, Lord, I forget that you are also the Lord of today—the project, the meeting, the church, the fleeting in-between that is right in front of me. Give me this day—this disordered in-between day—my daily bread and turn my well-intentioned mix-ups and messes into redeemable moments for you. In the name of the One who always gets it right . . . Amen.

# These Days

A phrase in a distinguished professional journal caught my eye. "These days are difficult times for ministry." Faster than a scream on Space Mountain, my mind blurted, "Duh! You betcha! Exactly! Here's a no-brainer! These *are* tough times for ministry. What genius wrote this?"

These days are difficult. But, what makes these days any different from other days? What makes them seem so very difficult? Haven't other generations faced difficult days? Of course they have. So, what's new? What's the climate? What's the scoop? The question remains . . . what makes *these days* uniquely difficult times for ministry in the Christian faith?

From Barna to Gallup, *Christianity Today* to *The Christian Century*, NBC *Nightly News* to FOX News, and *USA Today* to your local newspaper, the veiled answers seem to all be there. Yet, they hide before our very eyes like chameleons of truth blending in with our busy lives.

As a Christian leader, what resonates with you? What chameleons are you discovering? Here are a few of my random thoughts about ministry in *these days*. I hope they will stoke your reflective fire. Test them against your list.

*Globalization* – In a global neighborhood, where do we find community? With the advent of CNN and other round-the-clock news programming, I often seem to know more about my global neighborhood than the people next door.

*Technology* – Marvelous advancements now allow us to be fairly self-contained. We can travel the world without leaving our computer chair. We can acquire knowledge without personal encounter—obtaining data void of face-to-face dialogue which cuts off the necessity for relationships. We Instant Message, yet we sit alone at the keyboard without a handshake, hug, or human touch.

*Consumerism* – We too often worship the *god of good stuff!* We devour the liturgy of sale, clearance, and close-out. We fill empty lives with trinkets, bobbles, and the trivial bling of our day. The Holy Eucharist becomes burgers and fries as we gather at the Sacred Food Court. The Retailer is our shepherd; we shall not want. The Mall is our temple; attendance is better than ever.

*Post-Modernism* – Modernity reigns. Traditional Judeo-Christian institutional pillars crumble; the church is faced with a new frontier of ministry for which it is increasingly ill-equipped. No longer do we have the luxury to wonder, "How do we keep them down on the farm after they've seen *Parië?*" We must now contend with, "How do we keep them faithful to Jesus, after they've seen MTV?" We go to church, but the secularizing modernity of our culture is a 24/7 influence in our homes. It is as common as running water and as powerful as atomic energy.

You and I both know that there is more. Much more! Without a doubt, these are difficult days *for* ministry and to be *in* ministry. Yet, in spite of this, Christian leaders are called to be faithful. We are called to *these days*—the daunting age in which we live. We are called to listen up, pray up, and speak up in a tainted culture that is filled with a curious, up-to-the-minute citizenry. Ministry life has never been so bleak and so invigorating all at the same time!

## *The Leader's Prayer:*

God of *these days* . . . throw open the flood gates of understanding, knowledge, and concern. Teach me about *these days*. Prepare me for the unknown. School me in the disposition of this emerging generation. Tutor me in your imaginative state-of-the-art plan to use me. Quicken my spirit to be a fast learner, raring-to-go responder, and contemporary Christian leader worth your investment. In the name of the One who sits at your right hand and intercedes for me in *these days* . . . Amen.

# The Hunkie Cooper Principle

You don't have a clue who Hunkie Cooper is, do you? If you do, I'm impressed! If you don't, that's okay. Nevertheless, let me fill in a few Hunkie Cooper blanks for most of you.

Hernandez James (Hunkie) Cooper is a 5' 9" 190 pound former wide receiver and linebacker for the Arizona Rattlers, an Arena Football League perennial power house. Hunkie is a star. He is a Rattlers and Arena Football legend. As an offensive force, he is the AFL all-time leader in all-purpose yards and kickoff returns. He is the all-time leader in five Rattlers statistical categories. As a linebacker, he darted back and forth across the condensed AFL playing field and popped opponents like an angry gnat with a sledge hammer. He is a two-time recipient of the Ironman of the Year award and voted AFL MVP in 1993. In 2005 the Rattlers retired Hunkie Cooper's #14—the first number ever retired by the team. Hunkie loved the game of football and played it with a heart the size of the Grand Canyon. Yet outside of Arena Football League circles, he is little known and seldom recognized.

Several years ago in a television broadcast of a playoff game between the Arizona Rattlers and the Colorado Crush (the team owned by legendary quarterback John Elway), one of the announcers paid Hunkie a huge compliment. He said, "Hunkie doesn't have all of the skills that he used to, but he still makes big plays. He is a great leadership presence for the younger players. He really invests himself in helping the younger players learn the game."

Right then and there, it hit me. This is *The Hunkie Cooper Principle for Church and Ministerial Leadership*. Most of us are little known. We are seldom recognized outside our local communities, families, and denominational church circles. We may have racked up some pretty hefty ministry yardage, can still run pretty smoothly from one obligation to another on our modest church playing field, and can still pop out a fairly decent lesson for Sunday mornings. But the Hunkie Cooper Principle reminds me that there is something more to ministry than *my* performance. There are time-honored and significant intangibles that make great football players. Some of these very same intangibles help to fashion top-notch spiritual leaders as well. The Hunkie Cooper Principle reminds me to:

1. Love the game (of ministry).

2. Love the Founder of the game.

3. Play with a big heart.

4. Not worry about the size of the playing field.

5. Keep giving—even when age steals some energy and years of toil diminish a little skill.

6. Sustain youthful enthusiasm.

7. Not allow a lack of recognition to lessen your efforts.

8. Remember, your outlook determines your output.

9. Not forget that your leadership presence emerges from both your *doing* and your *being*.

10. Invest in younger colleagues—help them learn the craft of ministry.

These leadership intangibles are time-honored and just a few of the hidden imprints etched in a God-invested life and ministry.

And, that's The Hunkie Cooper Principle for Ministerial Leadership.

### *The Leader's Prayer:*

God of Surprising Images . . . keep showing me how to lead your church. Break into my routine with fresh visions for leadership, new examples of your desires for me, eye-openers of enthusiasm that keep me motivated. Open me up to the fullness of your thinking and set my feet in holy motion. In the name of the Captain of my Faith . . . Amen.

# *Somewhat Lost*

Did you ever get "somewhat" lost? Do you know what I mean? Are you familiar with this concept? If not, here it is. You jump into the car and hike out. You thought that you knew where you were going. I mean you *really* thought that you knew where you were going. But somehow you got a little off course, a little turned around, a little mixed up . . . a bit detained. [Men understand what I'm saying here. We never get *actually* lost . . . only *somewhat* lost.]

Truth be told, some of us have a better nose for north, south, east, and west than others. For instance, Victoria, my wife, is a much better navigator than I am. She has a built-in sense of direction. This *usually* keeps us out of trouble. She can tell her northeast from her southwest nearly every time. I, on the other hand, am a bit directionally challenged. I can find my way out of the driveway, but from there on things can get a little hairy.

Just recently, on one of my ministry excursions, I got *a bit turned around*. [This phrase is traveler's code language. It means that I am dreadfully lost but don't have to admit to it.] I could read the signs. I knew exactly where I was. But, what I desperately wanted to know was "Where should I be?" I don't handle *somewhat* lost very well.

After my frustration frenzy, I realized that asking "Where should I be?" is not all that bad of a question. As a matter of fact, it is pretty good query for pondering material. So, I ponder.

My ministry work takes me to more than forty congregations in any given year. When you add in conferences, seminars, and special events, I get the opportunity to experience a host of diverse speakers, an array of preaching styles, and a variety of pulpit/ podium mannerisms. Frankly, some of these oratory experiences are much better than others. So recently on this ministerial journey, I have been pondering the topic of effective preaching. While I recognize that there are books, courses, and all kinds of self-helps on this subject, I respectfully offer the following as an American Automobile Association (AAA) TripTik for a where-should-we-be-in-preaching travel plan:

> 1. Be in the Scriptures - rummage around for the fresh truth in God's Word.
>
> 2. Be in the Story - paint the heart, soul, and mind

of the biblical characters.

3.   Be in the Pew - grab relevancy, where today's people live, work, and struggle.

4.   Be in the Spirit – embrace God's presence, power, and purpose in your preaching.

In the frenzy of ministry life, it is easy to get a bit turned around, a little mixed up, or even slightly off track. But as I ponder the high calling of preaching—communicating the Gospel message—I am convinced that we are never to be lost . . . even somewhat. Staying in the Scriptures, in the story, in the pew, and in the Spirit keeps the proclamation journey headed in the right direction and precisely on course.

## The Leader's Prayer:

Lord of the Road and the Message . . . fill my wandering heart and mind with your story. Keep me on the road, between the lines, and headed your direction. Rid my prideful ego of the failure to stop and ask you for directions. Map out my words that I might always be on course with you. No shortcuts. No detours. No lost journeys. Direct your help and hope and faith and truth through my mind, my heart, and my lips. Pass it on to those who gather to listen—the hurting, the spiritually homeless, and the tattered saints who are often *somewhat* lost.  In the name of the One who was frequently on the road and *always* on message . . . Amen.

# Are We There Yet?

We climbed into the car, buckled seat belts, fixed mirrors, and launched the *we-are-off-on-a-trip-fine-tuning* procedure.

Our four girls wiggled around, positioning themselves to be sure that there was just enough room for them and *all* of the essentials—dolls, blankets, pillows, small toys, travel games, coloring books, crayon box, stuffed animals, and anything else that they and my wife deemed essential.

Satisfied that all was set, I cranked the engine, shifted from park to drive, pulled out, and headed down Route 30. About ninety seconds into our three-hour jaunt, one of our little brood chirped, "Daddy, are we there yet?" Lovingly, as I choose to remember it, I responded, "No, Honey. We just left home. We have a long, long way to go."

I must confess, the next fifty-five times this foreseeable question was peeped during the succeeding two hours, fifty-eight minutes, and thirty seconds; it did start to get on my nerves. I became aggravated and blurted out secret replies in my mind. Thoughts like, "Helloooo! How can we possibly be there? We've just driven five minutes and its 163 miles to Grandma's house!" Or "I don't think so! Why in the world are you asking me again? Didn't I just hear that four minutes ago?" Or "Just BE quiet! I'll tell you when we get there!" However, before any of these mental bad-daddy replies could come out of my mouth, God reminded me about the nature and perspective of the questioner. The query came from the understanding, reasoning, and patience of a child. With this awareness, my response needed to be in kind: loving, simple, enduring, gentle, and thoughtful.

Of late, the tables have been turned. I find myself calling out to God from the backseat.

I want to be there! I want to know why it takes *forever* to arrive. Some days I don't think that we'll ever get there. I get tired of the ride. I get bored at coloring in the same old books. I get frustrated with the same old stuffed teddy bears. I get anxious about the journey. And I get a bit aggravated with the rest of the family members in the car. "Abba, are we there yet?"

I'm not certain if God has any secret replies in his mind. I am, however, increasingly certain that the Almighty continues to know the nature and perspective of the questioner. The One who is all wisdom recognizes how many times I have the understanding, reasoning, and patience of a child. He knows that I have not arrived. He knows that the church has not arrived. He knows that the rest of my brothers and sisters in the family of God have not arrived. It is not a news flash to God that the church and I are not there yet.

Now, here is the amazing part. He doesn't scold me. My Father doesn't tell me how silly and immature I am for not comprehending the length of the journey. He doesn't even seem to be impatient with me. And even when I am testy with the church, the One who sits in the driver's seat is calm. My Father tenderly looks into my eyes, and without a word, I know there is still a long, long way to go. And, that's okay.

Yes, I'm not there yet. The church is not there yet. Praise be to God for his patience, his wisdom, and that we are not making this trip alone.

## *The Leader's Prayer:*

God of Patience . . . thank you for being behind the wheel. Thank you for understanding when I am immature, impatient, and impossible. Forgive my childish desire "to be there" in a hurry. There is so much to see, to learn, and to appreciate. Help me to rest in your presence, to enjoy the ride, and to be taught by you. In the name of the One who traveled well . . . Amen.

# Play It Again, Sam

*Casablanca* is one of the all-time hits of Hollywood—a silver screen classic. Humphrey Bogart. Ingrid Bergman. Love. Adventure. Emotion. Power. Romance. Intrigue. *Casablanca* has all of the "right stuff." It certainly is a flick with generational staying power. Ahhh . . . [sigh of nostalgic reminiscence] they sure don't make'em like that anymore.

Have you seen the movie? Do you remember the scene where Ilsa (Bergman) requests *the song*? Sam touches the keys and the melody of "As Time Goes By" fills the club. Rick (Bogie) slips into the scene. Heatedly, he reminds Sam that he never wants to hear that song again. Almost instantly Rick spots Ilsa. In that moment, the world changes. Everything is different. Anticipation saturates the air. Rick's heart wells up with passion as he delivers one of the most memorable lines in all of motion picture history. With his notable Bogie-like manner, he merely says, "Play it again, Sam." Wow!

So, what does all of this have to do with leadership? Not much, except that it is a great way to repeat some *play-it-again* principles for ministry—ones that seem to have generational staying power.

How can we develop into the kind of Christian leaders that God needs in order to create spiritually healthy environments for his people to grow, to thrive, and to fulfill his mission? As you contemplate your own list of what it will take, please consider the following as having *Casablanca-like* traits for getting the job done.

God needs leaders who will:

- Provide strong guidance with a gentle spirit.

- Place Kingdom goals above personal agendas.

- Promote less *I* and more *we*.

- Blend authority and authenticity with humor and humility.

- Design a congregational ministry umbrella that preserves the best of the old and shelters the best of the new.

- Balance looking ahead with looking back, looking in with looking out, and looking around with looking up.

- Build up rather than tear down.

- Turn chaos and conflict into victory and vitality.

This leadership vision is attainable, but only if we, as God-honoring leaders, want it. Leaders themselves must long to be "spiritually healthy." Successful leaders learn to network with one another for encouragement and mutual support. They yearn to further the Kingdom of God. Those out front must aspire to produce a robust New Testament church environment. Apart from this, I fear that the church will be doing business as usual.

I'm not Bogie, but my heart does well up with passion for the church. I fear that unless we play it again and again and again, *as time goes by* we will be doomed . . . settling for what we want out of *our* church rather than what God wants out of *his* church.

This leadership initiative will take courage, trust, and generous portions of grace; but we can get there from here. We *can* do it!

Play it again—that leadership song that never grows old. Play it again—that song that warms my soul. Play it again—that song that fills my life with passion and purpose and joy. Play it again, Sam—that God's *tomorrow-church* may come today.

### The Leader's Prayer:

Jehovah Jireh, Great God of Provision . . . sing to me. Sing again and again. Play for me tunes of vision, of hope, and of breathtaking dreams for your church. Play it again and again until I get it—until I fully understand who you are calling me to be and what you are calling me to do. Fill me with your passion, your power, and your purpose that I will develop into a leader who is pleasing in your sight. In the name of the One most pleasing . . . Amen.

# Glory Days

A number of years ago, I was invited to be the guest speaker at a series of renewal services at the Frost Bite Community Church near Anchorage, Alaska. (The name and location of the church have been altered to protect the *almost* innocent!) I like to arrive early for these events. This gives me an opportunity to meet some of the key church leaders and "get the lay of the land." So, I made travel arrangements to facilitate arriving on Saturday afternoon in plenty of time to have an evening meal with some of the prominent church members.

During our dinner discussion, I was instructed that one of the deacon couples would be taking me home to stay with them for the week. After supper, an attractive couple in their early seventies approached me. They quickly identified themselves as Jack and Jill—my host and hostess for the week. As we made our way to the restaurant door, Jill inquired, "Would you like to take a run by church on the way home?" I responded with a quick, "Sure."

Following a brief tour of the sanctuary and fellowship hall, my hosts took me directly to their Sunday school room. We no more had set foot in the room, when Jill motioned to me. "Come here. I'd like to show you a picture." She pointed me in the direction of a large picture which conspicuously hung on the back wall of the classroom. As I approached the picture, I recognized that it was an old photograph of families gathered at what appeared to be a picnic.

"That was our class forty years ago," Jill said. "We had fifty or sixty in our class, plus all the kids, too." She paused, glanced at Jack, choked back a faint sigh, and continued. "Now we might get ten or twelve in our class. Our children have all moved away. There aren't any young people in our church any more. Church attendance is less than half of what our Sunday school class used to be." With deep longing in her eyes, she paused for a second time. "I wish we could be like that again."

Jill yearned for the glory days of her church. She and Jack wanted nothing more than for things to be the way they used to be.

This is a common state of affairs for many congregations. The picture on the wall is a bit different. The words come out slightly altered. But the storyline and longing are pretty much the same . . . *How do we recapture the Glory Days in our church?*

As church leaders, we must come to grips with this kind of congregational lament. Here are a few tools that you can "get" to assist in addressing this recurrent yearning:

- *Get Perspective*: A lamenting search for old church glory is like seeing a mirage. It is real enough to see but never real enough to have.

- *Get Focused*: The picture on your Sunday school room wall is a snapshot in time. It is longing for the 1957 Studebaker that you will never again drive.

- *Get Beyond the Grief*: Every day spent looking at the picture on the wall is one more day of grieving the loss rather than pursuing the future.

- *Get Context*: What was, was! What is, is! So, explore your congregation's changing context for ministry. The thing(s) that God called you to do and to be forty years ago will most likely not be identical to what God *is* calling you to do and to be today.

- *Get Praying*: Jabez called out to God with openness to the future. "Oh, that You would bless me indeed, and enlarge my territory, that Your hand would be with me, and that You would keep *me* from evil, that I may not cause pain!" (1Chronicles 4:10 NKJV). And, God granted the request.

If you are a leader in a church searching for its glory days, you may need to take a quick glance backward; but time is best spent focusing ahead. The best glory days are not born of lament but of hard work. They are not old reproductions but new realities.

## *The Leader's Prayer:*

God of Yesterday and Today . . . I celebrate yesterday—the glory days, when all seemed good and we gathered at the park for fried chicken, potato salad, and cherry pie. I rejoice in today—the vision days, when we can come together around a new tomorrow, a fresh dream, and the image of a brand new picture for the church. Protect us from longing for the past and failing to seize moments in the now and opportunity for the future. In the name of the One who is timeless—who is yesterday's glory, today's hope, and tomorrow's vision . . . Amen.

# Serving in the Shadows

I once served in a congregation where I followed a pastor of thirty-eight years. Notice that I said, "Once." Once was enough! This was a million-dollar experience which cost me more than I could have ever imagined. I battled stress. I gained weight. I misplaced focus. I lost sleep. I accumulated advocates. I distanced critics. I abandoned my own gifting. I became *the savior* (from the old way) for some parishioners and *the devil* (of change) for others as I served in the shadows of a previous leader without a clue about the dynamics of these kinds of circumstances.

I weathered this episode gaining a life-experience Ph.D. from the University of Ministry Survival. I learned a lot, but I wish that I had had some idea, some inkling, some clue, some hint, of how difficult it was going to be. I wish that I had known how to handle all of the sundry stuff that came my way. Regrettably, I continue to see leadership transition gaffes happen over and over again as I work with congregations. So, in case you ever find yourself replacing a beloved previous pastor or strong-natured deacon or personality-plus board chair, and before the waves of controversy come crashing in all around you, I want to pass along some tips for ministry leadership survival.

1. Assist the congregation in attaining closure with the previous leader. Whenever possible, hold a ministry celebration to recognize the ministry achievements and contributions of the previous leader. And formally bring their leadership period to an end.

2. Facilitate a healthy congregational understanding of the new relationship with its former leader. I strongly urge the former leader to take the lead in instructing the congregation about its new relationship with him/her. The former leader should "pass the mantle" of leadership to the new person in charge and direct the congregation to the new leader.

3. Make sure that you and the previous leader are "playing off the same page." There should be an unambiguous and mutually agreed upon understanding regarding the new relationship. Any hint of a problem should be promptly discussed with appropriate congregational and/or judicatory

leadership.

4. Be intentional about defining who you are and how you intend to function. Educate the congregation regarding spiritual gifting and leadership style. Talk about the gifts and style of the former leader. Demonstrate how his/her gifts and style might be similar to or different from the gift package, skill set, and leadership style that you bring to the position of leadership. Also, orient the congregation to the fact that these gifts are neither "good" nor "bad," but they *are* different.

5. Build strong relationships with key congregational leaders. Capture a sense of their vision for the congregation. Talk with them about your vision. Begin to make helpful connections between their vision and your vision. Assist them in developing and owning a congregational vision based on an appreciation for the rich heritage of the past, the fresh realities of the present, and their common hopes and dreams for a vital future.

6. Love people through the transition. Let them talk freely about the past and lovingly nudge them toward the future.

7. Endure! Exercise patience as you give persons the needed time and space to latch on to your new leadership style.

Serving in the shadows of a former beloved, strong-natured, or charismatic leader can be a tricky assignment. But, with an ample dose of God's grace, just a little help from your friends, and a head start on what to expect, it can be a meaningful and well-spent season in ministry.

## *The Leader's Prayer:*

God of Change and Light . . . there is no shadow of turning with you. Anchor me in the stormy seas of transition. With you at the helm, teach me to help your people see beyond the squall of change to the marvelous light of a promising future. Guide me through these rough waters to the shore of tomorrow. And be blessed by how this voyage is being made. In the strong name of the One who mastered the sea . . . Amen.

# Things to Keep

My father is a Pack Rat. If there was an Olympic Pack Rat Marathon, my dad would certainly be favored. He would accumulate, accrue, gather, amass, and horde his way to the finish line. At the events end, he would ascend the coveted podium, bow his head, and have Olympic Gold placed around his neck. Draped in the American Flag, (maybe more than one!) he would circle the stadium for a victory lap. Okay, so maybe I've overstated this a bit. Maybe he wouldn't get the Gold, but the Bronze is a lock!

Catch the picture here. The second story of my parent's Cape Cod is loaded. The three basement rooms are packed. The two-car garage—where one car barely fits—is jammed. This snapshot doesn't even address the main living area! There is stuff from owning a small grocery store in the 1950s; stuff from working

20-plus years at Studebaker's in South Bend, Indiana; stuff from serving on the town council; stuff from coaching my Little League baseball team; reading stuff; (Dad considers habitual junk mail as literature not to be taken lightly.); and, the ever present *I-might-need-that-some-day* stuff.

I've known about this malady for some time, but it wasn't an issue until just a few years ago. In light of some significant health concerns, my parents planned a major downsizing and move to Pennsylvania to live with us. So, the big questions became . . . What's trash? What's treasure? What gets packed? What gets pitched? What do you donate? What is important enough to keep?

This whole family episode has caused me to do some reflective thinking about downsizing—lightening life's load. It has caused me to consider making some critical judgments about what might need to go and what is important enough to keep.

Now, I have no clue what you have packed away in your ministry garage, scheduling basement, or emotional attic, but I am fairly clear that some things need to go and some need to stay. So, if you are in the mood to downsize, if you are motivated to cut the clutter in your life . . . go for it! Yet in all of the pitching, tossing, and shredding, I am asking you to consider salvaging some of these:

1. Keep a closet filled with well-used garments of integrity.

2. Keep a sack stuffed full of passion and compassion.

3. Keep several bags of humor.

4. Keep a carton of straightened out priorities.

5. Keep a case of good, up-to-date books.

6. Keep a huge container of solid Christ-honoring wisdom.

7. Keep a bundle of forgiveness.

8. Keep a box of courage.

9. Keep a trunk packed with meaningful ministry memories.

10. Keep space open for recreation, reflection, and renewal.

First-class leaders learn to downsize. So pitch the clutter. Dump the distractions. Clip the calendar. Slash the to-do list. Unload the disorder. Limit the interruptions. Get back to basics. Always remember the things to keep. Be the quality leader that God is calling you to be.

*The Leader's Prayer:*

Lord of Simplicity . . . lighten my load. Give me the gumption to rid myself and my leadership from dust-laden encumbrances—all the accumulated stuff that hinders my service to you. Show me what must go. Confirm what must stay. Reduce to bare bones my lofty views of self achievement. Simplify. Clean up. Clear out. Send me packing—light for travel with you. In the name of the One who instructed his disciples to pack light—to "Take no gold, nor silver, nor copper in your belts, no bag for your journey, nor two tunics, nor sandals, nor a staff." (Matthew 10:9-10 RSV) . . . Amen.

# Outside the Lines

Well, I've done it. I've descended to a new low. I've plunged into the pit of virtual illustration. I've tumbled into the net of cyberspace trivia. I have shamelessly adapted an email forward as the basis for this chapter.

We all get these things—annoying email forwards—from family and friends trying to be nice, cute, or make their particular point. Frankly, not many of these virtual annoyances grab my attention. When it comes to this form of junk mail, my take is that deleted is better than delighted. Yet intrigued by one of the titles and seeing that it was from a former parishioner, I opened it.

Considering the potential for church leadership, I have blatantly apprehended the pesky thing and reworked it for my sanctified purposes. Check out this thought-provoking riddle.

You are driving along on an untamed, windy, and stormy winter night, when your car passes a remote and lonely bus stop. As you slowly roll by, you glance out your window and see three people standing out in the wretched night. 1) An elderly woman—cold, haggard, frail, and appearing to be near death. 2) An old friend who once, in a heroic act, saved your life. Now sad, lost, and seemingly hopeless, he looks to you for help. 3) The woman of your dreams—alluring, charming, and stunningly beautiful. As your eyes meet, she appears to be calling out to you in the frigid night air. It is visibly clear that she is in despair and in immediate need of your rescue. (If you are female, please feel free at this point to insert "man of your dreams" with all of the suitable descriptive attributes and pronouns to follow.)

Here's the dilemma. Knowing that your car can only take one passenger, who would you rescue? Who would you choose? How would you resolve this weird and astounding moral/ethical/personal impasse?

You can assist the elderly lady and thus compassionately save her life. Should she go first? You could rescue your old friend and, in so doing, repay him for heroically saving your life. Should he be the one? Or, knowing that you may never find your perfect love again, you could snatch the moment, gallop to your prospective soul mate like Prince Charming, and whisk her away on your faithful white stallion securing your *happily-ever-after* future. Should she be your choice?

Apparently, this predicament was posed as an interview question to potential employees as a part of their employment screening process. Out of 200 applicants, there was only one hired. What did he say? What would you say? Think about it. Try to color outside the lines.

The winning respondent simply said, "I would give my car keys to my old friend and instruct him to take the elderly woman to the hospital for treatment. Then I would stay behind at the bus stop with the woman of my dreams and wait for the bus." [This illustration has been posted on various websites. I have adapted it from the posting on: http://www.dreamriverdesign.com/ratn/ tests/busstop.html. Also posted at: http://www.life-support-usa. com/riddles5.html.]

As church leaders—Christian women and men who are called to lead in these very difficult and transitional times—let me urge you to color outside the lines. Look for all of the faith-honoring, *win-win* solutions that can be found. In and of itself this will not guarantee success, but it will demonstrate your personal willingness to fashion potential resolutions rather than manufacture conventionally construed obstacles.

## *The Leader's Prayer:*

God of Deep Simplicity . . . move my thinking beyond the suspiciously obvious—the kind of run of the mill thinking that keeps us stuck. Teach me to keep on probing for your budding possibilities. Remind me that it's okay to color outside the lines, think outside the box, and move beyond the predictable. In the humdrum of our business-as-usual church life, lead me to unforeseen endings, startling finales, and the creative twists in your profoundly simple wisdom. In the name of the One who commonly colored outside the expected lines . . . Amen.

# *Dancing with Danger*

O kay. Here it is. Confession time. I like to dance! There, I've said it. The word is out. Now you know. And for your further information, I used to be good! Recently, an arthritic knee (old football injury) and chronic chubbiness (youthful eating habits) have tended to slow me down some. But I still delight in a bit of music-inspired motion.

A number of years ago, when I was in the pastorate, our family attended a wedding for a niece and her new husband. During the reception, I was on the dance floor with my oldest daughter, Kimberly. Her boyfriend (now husband) was standing there taking it all in. Soon his head began shaking from side to side in a disbelieving motion. Observing his reaction, my wife quizzed him, "Don't you like to see your girlfriend dancing with her daddy?" He respectfully shot back, "She's not dancing with her daddy. She's dancing with *my* pastor!"

Today we all laugh about this little family episode. But apparently, faced with the reality at hand, this *dancing thing* was a novel and quite dangerous concept for my new son-in-law-to-be.

For many of us, dancing in the church is not the taboo that it once was. The days of all musical motion being evil are pretty well past. (I note here that modesty in motion is still in good Christian taste.) However, truth be told, dancing in the church can still be hazardous. When we dance, there are those—both inside and outside the church—who still chitchat. It happened to Jesus and it can happen to us.

Jesus danced with danger when he spoke openly with a Samaritan woman, when he protected the woman caught in adultery, and when he took up with tax collectors. He danced with danger when he dared to lead with authority, when he failed to give a disclaimer to his high calling, when he washed the feet of his friends, when he faced contempt with silence, when he romped around with a peculiar group of ragtag fishermen, and when he chose to hang out with a few questionable female companions.

Yet the music played on. The Composer grinned. The orchestra kicked it up a notch. The left out, the over-looked, and the rejected all joined in. But there were those who watched and wagged their heads and viewed his steps as a new and perilous jig.

For many of us in ministry, moving to the new rhythms of leadership is certainly risky business. We may indeed find ourselves dancing with danger on a number of untouchable and time-honored occasions. When strong leaders seek to put mission above polity, some won't hear the music. When daring leaders abandon programming and goal setting for gift-based ministry and Spirit-led passion, there will be those who will claim that the music is all wrong. When courageous leaders move onto the dance floor with the disenfranchised, broken, hurting, uneducated, racially diverse, and denominationally unpedigreed, some will say that there is no music at all.

But the music still plays! The Composer still smiles. And for those who dare to do so, dancing with danger still moves the church.

### *The Leader's Prayer:*

Lord of the Dance . . . send *your* music down! Make my heart jump. Put the spring back into my step. Make my feet move and prance and skip and glide and leap for joy! Teach me the new rhythms of leadership so that I might always be in step with you. Keep me in perfect motion with your song. In the name of the One who never missed a beat . . . Amen.

# Do You Get It?

I get around to a lot of churches in the course of my ministry. This provides me the rare opportunity to see what works and what doesn't. Frankly, I've concluded that some congregations *get it* and some don't. Some congregations, either by conscious design or by intuitive revelation, key into the authentic connectional dynamics that engage new persons. Other congregations suffer the triple threat of degeneration—stumble, fumble, and fall into deep patterns of decline.

Let me paint you a word Picasso to illustrate. On a recent Sunday morning my wife and I headed off to church. As we entered the church narthex (Christianeze for church entry way) no one greeted us. We stood in that icy climate—both physical and relational—for more than twenty minutes with no one present saying a word to us! Fifteen to twenty people milled around in the same area waiting for a Sunday school class, which was meeting in the sanctuary, to dismiss. These *friendly* folks were clearly enjoying their visiting with each other. They seemed to be a sociable bunch, but Victoria and I just stood off to one side very much alone. We were literally ignored!

I was compelled to wonder, w*here is the "Hey!"* . . . *the "Good Morning!"* . . . *the "Hi, good to have you with us for worship."* . . . *the "Hi, my name's Bill, I don't think that we've met before."* . . . *the "Good to see you."* One of these, any of these, even a smile or a nod would have been nice. But, there was nothing. They didn't get it!

At an appropriate time during the worship service, the pastor introduced us as the District Executive and his wife. He expressed how good it was that we were able to visit them this morning. Wow, what a change. Immediately after the service, throngs of people flocked around us, shook hands, chatted, smiled, laughed, and greeted us with genuine hospitality. One person even said, "I thought that was you out there in the narthex."

Though no words about these dynamics were spoken, the church's message was loud and clear. When I was identified as a Somebody, I was greeted with enthusiasm, warmth, and fellowship. When I was a mysterious Nobody—a nameless visitor loitering in the nippy narthex—I was overlooked, pushed to the social periphery, and disregarded as a non-entity. This message made me both sad and angry.

This church didn't get it! They didn't get the fact that you only get one chance to make a first impression. They didn't understand that their "ice-covered narthex message" that morning was ten times more powerful than the message that had come from the pulpit. They didn't fully grasp the hypocrisy of their greeting gaffe—the insider-outsider flip-flop—that occurred both before and after the service. They simply didn't get it.

So, who does get it? Who recognizes the key elements to making a relational connection with new folks? Here are four out-of-the-blue encounters that opened up my eyes. It sounds as if these folks really do get it. Check this out.

Wal-Mart gets it. They don't have a clue what a narthex is but they do put a greeter immediately inside the front door. You have to actually *try* to miss their greeting if you don't want one. Wal-Mart doesn't wait to see if you're a somebody or not. They don't wait to see if you're going to buy anything before they greet you. Their "Howdy!" is right up front. They want you to know that *you* and anybody that you brought along with you are important and welcome.

Waffle House gets it. In 1955 Waffle House opened its first restaurant in Avondale Estates, Georgia, serving its first cup of welcoming coffee. Today Waffle House serves more than 95 million cups of their blend of "java howdy" each year. Co-founder, Joe Rogers, Jr., seeks to operate by the advice given to him by his father: "Always treat your customers like family—greet them warmly, never take them for granted and always make them feel welcome by offering them a great cup of coffee." On my latest visit to Waffle House, three employees gave me a "Good Morning!

How'ya doin'!" before I ever reached my seat. That's exactly three more than the church I noted earlier.

Famous Dave's gets it. On a visit to Nashville, Victoria and I were encouraged to try a small local chain of *Legendary Pit Bar-B-Ques*. We soon knew why: good food; fair prices; and, a down home friendly atmosphere where even Yankees, like us, were made to feel at home. A laminated card displayed on every table read, "We operate our business by what we call the *FD Rule*. Treat others better than they expect to be treated. And we are firmly committed to the five values that are our name: Faith, Family, Friends, and Famous Food. Thank you for visiting our home . . . thanks for sharing time with us . . . God Bless!"

Jesus gets it. With arms open wide he extends a welcome to the somebodies and nobodies, the rich and poor, the black and white, the brown and yellow, the urban and rural, the regulars and first-timers, the young and old, the educated and illiterate, the beautiful and plain, the friends and strangers. He gets it. So should the leaders of his church.

## The Leader's Prayer:

Good morning, Lord . . . thank you for greeting me. Thanks for chatting with me when no one else seems to care. Thanks for making me a Somebody when inside I repeatedly feel like a Nobody. Thank you for welcoming me into your Kingdom and your church. Help me, as a church leader, to get it—to understand that Kingdom messages are proclaimed in many differing ways and to see that my smile and my conversation may be someone's narthex to your presence. Help me and my church create an inviting atmosphere for all who come seeking you. In the name of the One who welcomes everybody as Somebody . . . Amen.

# Beyond Charming

Advent is the festive period of expectancy which kicks off the Christmas season. As we all know, it is a fixed place in the Christian calendar when the church sets aside moments and events to reflect on and prepare for the celebration of the birth of the Christ Child—the mystery of the Incarnation and marvel of the Word becoming flesh, walking and talking and being right here among us. Literally, however, advent (small "a") simply means a coming into being or use. A statement like, "Bedtimes came much earlier before the advent of electricity" illustrates this basic meaning. In all cases, advent—regardless of whether or not it is capitalized—has to do with a coming, dawning, or arrival.

For many in the church, the highlight of the Advent season is the annual Children's Christmas Pageant—frequently a congregational ritual jam-packed with terry cloth livestock, a four-year-old shepherd who playfully sticks out his tongue at another shepherd, a posse of one-night-only angels with flimsy wire halos, glitzy Magi toting curiously gaudy gifts, a Mary who gazes into the manger with a finger in her nose [I've witnessed this one!], and a Joseph who nervously sneaks a wave to his mother. Not to be forgotten is the I've-Almost-Reached-Puberty Choir overflowing with yet-to-be singers and a dedicated director who deserves a jewel in her crown for even attempting to produce this thing. What a sight!

Please don't fault me for these observations. I'm not being critical. I love Christmas pageants; after all, I'm a grandfather! But permit me to use a common phrase from Simon Cowell of *American Idol* fame. "Let me be perfectly honest with you," this is what I have in fact seen and heard in my thirty-five-plus years of parenting, sixteen-plus years of grandparenting, and more years than I care to mention in both pew and pulpit.

Most of these annual children's programs are charming—some would say downright cute. And they are. But I want more. I long for more than charming, more than cute, more than terry cloth sheep and a multitude of one-night angels. I long for an advent—a significant appearance—of increasing substance. As a church leader, I long for the advent of wholesome change— a good-faith striving to reach our shifting culture for Christ. I long for the dawn of peace in our pews that are time and again battlegrounds for petty differences. I long for the arrival of a church community where members talk *with* each other rather than grumble *about* each other and where they refuse to nitpick at pastors and congregational leadership. I long for an influx of pastors who authentically tend their flock and for the coming of lay leaders who live out an incarnational presence of Christ.

Yes, my heart longs for the richness of an advent that is beyond charming—where authenticity is Mary, faithfulness is Joseph, Jesus rests in good and capable hands, and the audience sees that this story is beyond charming. It is for real!

### *The Leader's Prayer:*

God of Stunning Arrivals . . . send a new beginning. Send your church a fresh start. Send your people—those of us too frequently satisfied with charming—a late breaking, up-to-the-minute display of your glory. Open our senses to your splendor, your veracity, and your commands. Bring us to a new day in the church. Let the world see that your people are more than charming, more than cute, more than juvenile ritual, more than terry cloth saints. Instead, let the world see a people sold out to authentic healing and to genuine hope and to matchless grace . . . a people of nonstop love and generous new beginnings. In the name of the One who is the advent of all things new . . . Amen.

# A Forgotten Priority

Maggie appeared to have everything. She drove a new Mercedes Benz. Her home, located in one of the finest neighborhoods in the city, was clearly in the million dollar range. Designer clothing filled her closet. Country club luncheons, tennis lessons, and pool parties were her social habitat. Her children were good-looking, popular, and on the elementary school honor roll. Maggie's attorney husband, Bill, was respected, successful, and handsome. His business and life couldn't have been better. So, what's the problem here? Isn't this the *Mona Lisa* image of the American dream?

Here's the quandary. Maggie was having an extramarital affair. When she came for counseling, her life was in shambles—unraveling, being torn apart seam by seam. She was lonely, depressed, and filled with a mountain of guilt. While I certainly did not condone Maggie's actions—sin is sin—it was obvious that her situation was the sad result of being a forgotten priority in her husband's hectic life. Bill's constant litany of empty words and endless string of broken promises left Maggie hurt, hostile, and frantic for affection: yet she maintained the outward appearance of "having it all." While she may have fooled some, she did not have it all–nor did she have it all together. Furthermore, her exterior circumstances provided a suitable camouflage for her emptiness, pain, and sin.

A forgotten priority always takes its toll. This is true not only for the Bill's and Maggie's of the world; it is also true for the church.

Take, for example, the Extremely United Community Church. It appears to have everything. The congregation has a fashionable 21-passenger diesel van. Their facility is located in one of the finest sections of town—location, location, location. The remodeled sanctuary, state-of-the-art gymnasium, and one-of-a-kind family life center put it among the elite congregations in the surrounding area.

And, there's more. The choir room is filled with designer choir robes. The annual Sunday school picnic and monthly class parties are grand social gatherings. Members of the youth group are clean-cut, hard-working, intelligent, and headed for respectable denominational church colleges. The congregation's pastor is esteemed, successful, and appealing. The ministry couldn't be better. So, what's the problem here? Isn't this the *Mona Lisa* image of the perfect American church?

Here's the dilemma. Much of the church is involved in the periphery affairs of ministry. Church leadership has been blinded to a forgotten priority . . . evangelism—the *unbashful* sharing of the Good News found in Jesus. This simple ministry gaffe hounds the soul of the church and redirects a fundamental mission given by Christ. Yet, it goes mostly undetected, giving the exterior appearance that we have it all and have it all together.

It was to Zacchaeus—the wealthy "have it all" tax collector—that Jesus announced his main intention. He declared, "For the Son of man came to seek and to save the lost." (Luke 19:10 RSV) It was to *all* the disciples—subsequently to the church that would follow—that Jesus made known his chief objective. He unflinchingly broadcast this priority for the church, "Go therefore and make disciples of all nations." (Matthew 28:19 RSV) What happened? There seems to be a constant litany of empty words and endless string of broken promises for not doing evangelism—great sounding excuses for why we do not "go and make disciples." The church has developed a variety of justifications: too busy . . . in the middle of a building project . . . don't feel comfortable sharing . . . think evangelism is best done by a few gifted professionals . . . are deeply vested in other *important* ministries . . . the church is too large already . . . and there are some among us who really don't believe in evangelism in the first place.

Evangelism has become a forgotten priority in much of contemporary church life—an unspoken and unwanted pregnancy in the family of God. It leaves this leader wondering how we will ever make disciples if persons aren't being challenged to first make a decision to follow Jesus. How will Jesus' mission be fulfilled if his chosen instrument of proclamation—the church—buries itself in unwillingness, silence, or minutia?

A forgotten priority *always* takes its toll.

### *The Leader's Prayer:*

God of *Good News* . . . praise you for the *Good News*—the life-transforming news in Jesus. Help me to face up to the challenge. Rally round your leaders and your church and help us to embrace the priority to broadcast your goodness, your mercy, your grace, and your love—the *Good News* so clearly seen in your Son, Jesus. In the name of the One who never forgot his priority . . . Amen.

# Rough Times

All leaders face rough times. Sooner or later, things get tough. They spin out of control. Everything suddenly seems to be uphill. It is never a matter of *if* rough times will come, but *when*!

As I meet with leaders across denominational lines at ecumenical gatherings, I am more and more reminded that the specific name of our denomination or church network doesn't really matter any more. Many of us are facing parallel issues. The forecast for rough times is right in front of us. It's as predictable as rain in April.

I quickly confess that I do not possess the answers to a lot of the complex questions and thorny struggles that face the church today. All the same, I would like to pose some common commitments that leaders can make for enduring these rough times. While these commitments will not solve all of our ecclesiastical woes, they will help keep us process-oriented, solution-based and on the move toward godly resolve. So, as we see how much spandex is in the fabric of our lives, as we arm wrestle for the coveted Polity Trophy, and as we doggedly muster allies for the Battle of Ideology, please consider this:

- Commit to Not Over-Reacting: This is not the first time that the Church of Jesus Christ has faced rough times. It will not be the last. Controversy is no stranger to the church. Check out Acts 6 or Acts 15. There are sandpaper moments, choppy junctures, and watershed interludes throughout Christian history. These defining episodes occur when the people of God must clarify who they are, what they believe, and where God is calling them to go.

- Commit to Prayer and Scripture: Prayer and Scripture are the twin citadels of discernment. Here we discover godly clarity, godly wisdom, and godly peace.

- Commit to Speaking the Truth in Love: This is the leader's biblical mandate. It is the Spirit-led guide for communication. It is our ultimate control in rough times. When deep, raw emotional energy runs high, all too often truth-in-love speaking flees the scene. However, deep conviction and powerful passion do not have to be love-less proclamations.

- Commit to Participate in the Decision-Making Process: Stay in the game. Resist the urge to bail or run or simply get fed up and flee the scene. A premature exit from the process forfeits your voice at the final decision-making table.

There is no doubt. These are rough times—days of historical significance for the church and people of faith. The church needs its leaders to hold fast, to listen well, to speak with loving conviction, and to endure persecution.

So, hold fast. The church needs you. You are a prize! You will help determine what the 21ˢᵗ Century will become. You will help determine how future generations will come to see and know Christ.

### The Leader's Prayer:

God of ALL Times . . . you know both the storm and the calm. You are Lord of the rough and windy sea—the water of change that frightens us, tosses us from side to side, and seems to endanger our very existence. You are Lord of the warm, sandy beach and quiet shore—the shoreline of peace that assures us of being grounded and safe and at home again. Lord, speak. Speak words of encouragement, wisdom, and vision. In these rough days of uproar in the church, grant me—and all your leaders—the calming reassurance of your abiding presence with us. Hold my hand and lead me into the next tomorrow. In the name of the One with nail-pierced hands . . . Amen.

# Kindergarten Leadership

On a visit to the area where I had previously served in ministry, a young girl (twelve or thirteen years of age) scurried across the front of the noisy sanctuary to greet me. She blurted out, "Hi, my name's Shelly. Do you remember me?"

I paused, flashed a clueless grin, and promptly disclosed my ignorance. "Sorry," I confessed. "Please remind me who you are."

"Shelly Johnson!" she spouted. "You married my Mom and Dad." She launched into an impetuous discourse about her parents, her school, and her life. Then, as quickly as she had appeared, she was gone! Poof! See ya! Out of here! Her life was movin' on!

Let me fill in some blanks of this story for you. Shelly was the offspring of Rudy and Edna, both of whom I had baptized and married. Their meeting was an unlikely one. Both Rudy and Edna had been involved in unhealthy lifestyles and lived at a great distance from the Lord's desire for each of their lives. Yet God was faithful. After coming to Christ individually, he brought them together, as a couple, in a remarkable way. It wasn't until years later that I learned I had played a significant role in their return to Christ and the church.

Edna confided in me about Rudy's turning point. It seems that one afternoon, while walking across the parking lot of the local supermarket, I called out to Rudy and engaged him in a simple how's-it-going conversation. She told me that he never forgot that exchange. I was the leader and *the leader* had called him by name and dared to talk to him!

In a separate conversation Rudy told me about Edna's turning point. It seems that I showed up at the hospital Emergency Room in the middle of the night to check in on one of her dearest friends who had just overdosed. According to his account *the leader* had come to see Edna's friend—a societal nonentity—who wasn't even a member of the church. Then he stayed around through the stomach pumping, vulgar outbursts and uncontrollable shaking just to be sure that this cherished friend was okay. [While these names are changed, the story is true.]

Please hear me. My purpose in telling this story is not to make something of myself. The truth is that I didn't even remember talking to Rudy that day in the parking lot. And although I remember being in the hospital Emergency Room, I don't remember any of the gruesome details from that night.

The reason I share this story is because seminary—the primary source of most ministry training—doesn't really teach us the significant dynamics that leaders need to know about effective fundamental ministry. This is not intended to be a slap at seminaries. It is not a cheap shot at higher education. Most institutions do a fine job of classical ministry training. However, a good number of them leap over the practical and dive right into the theological and philosophical. They often miss basic elementary truths of ministry. Some of the most important ministry lessons have been taught in classrooms without walls and in unscripted lectures by lay persons who have no clue that they were actually teaching at all.

Here are five Kindergarten Leadership Lessons I picked up from life-instructors like Rudy and Edna:

> 1. Parking lots make wonderful mission fields.

> 2. As a spiritual leader, people listen to you even when you're not talking.

> 3. When people tell their faith stories to their children, everybody benefits.

> 4. Some of life's greatest teachers don't hold degrees.

> 5. My best ministry consists of a few well-

intentioned, and somewhat unconscious, acts bathed in God's power and grace.

Seminary was great, but I missed a few things. Much of God's curriculum regarding effective ministry came much later. How about you?

## *The Leader's Prayer:*

Lord of the Parking Lot . . . praise you for watching over ordinary places. Thank you for simple lessons. Hone my skills so that I might be an authentic leader wherever you call. Thank you for sending teachers my way. Bless them and send new ones—the educated and uneducated alike—that I might continue to learn and be trained in your ways. In the name of the One who learned at the synagogue and at the foot of a carpenter's bench as well . . . Amen.

# Honk If You Love Jesus

Summer is great! The sun makes its annual migration northward, shoves spring aside, and infuses neighborhoods with balmy breezes and sidewalk lemonade stands. Since I live near Hershey, Pennsylvania, this balmy breeze phenomenon is especially good news. With the push of a button, my car window glides down and the sweet aroma of chocolate floats in and fills my world. (I must admit, however, that when the wind blows in the *wrong* direction, we get a rich whiff of the farm fresh fragrance formed by the milk-producing animals grazing just down the road. And it isn't chocolate!)

This warm chocolate bouquet wafting through the air, and thousands of visitors descending on Hershey Park, reminds me that this is not simply summer; it is also tourist season; and with tourist season comes bumper sticker season!

Bumper stickers are an automotive art form. These rolling billboards advertise political preferences, personal views on meaningless topics, bad attitudes, sports team alliances, school pride, and the individual expressions of theology or philosophy of life. Check out this batch of chrome commercials:

- *Come to Jesus. But keep your Distance!*

- *We're all dysfunctional; get over it!*

- *Eat well, stay fit, die anyway.*

- *Live for God. No Regrets.*

- *Caution: Driving under the influence of the Holy Spirit.*

- *When all else fails, lower your standards.*

- *If you can walk on water, call me.*

- *If you're living like there is no God, you'd better be right!*

- *If you can read this, you annoy me.*

- *Honk if you love Jesus.*

Though somewhat fascinated by them, bumper-sticker declarations are not really my thing. Fender faith, bumper believing, and vinyl evangelism have seldom impacted my life. I'm not here to criticize those who are compelled to witness in this way. In our culture, it does take a certain amount of courage to lay your faith on the bumper. Yet I can't help but wonder how much good it actually does.

In this day and age, it seems to me that the deep cry of the human spirit is for a faith that adheres to real life, confusing circumstances, and shaken values, much more than bumpers. Seekers in this postmodern age are looking for a faith that cements itself to conviction, holds fast when you can't figure it all out, and attaches to the very core of their being. They are looking for a faith that bonds broken relationships and fortifies marriages . . . for a faith that holds things together when cancer calls . . . for a faith that fuses justice, peace, grace, joy, and mercy . . . for a faith that is fastened to everyday life . . . for a faith where words and deeds organically stick together.

*Honk if you love Jesus*—the mother of all sacred bumper stickers— is a meager substitute for a personal conversation with a friend about your faith and trust in Jesus. *Honk if you love Jesus* can't hold a candle to working side by side with a victim of a devastating hurricane to restore their home. *Honk if you love Jesus* can't measure up to a compassionate hug when personal tragedy beats down health's door. *Honk if you love Jesus* may evoke a "beep" on the road; however, it rarely stirs a passing driver's heart to make the decision to follow Christ.

So if you're in a hurry and need to pass me on the road, go ahead and honk; but other than that, stick to the basics—love your neighbors, serve those in need, drive home the message of Jesus' love; in so doing, those closest to you will know your commitment to him extends beyond your bumper.

## The Leader's Prayer:

God of Compassion . . . enlarge my territory and my witness. Link my words and my deeds in such a way so those around me recognize that my faith and my God are real. Shield me from easy witnessing. Fill me with a growing concern for those around me who are in need—the ones for whom Jesus gave his life and sees fit to put into my path. In the name of the One we are urged to honk for—the One who strolled the roadway doing good . . . Amen.

# Gullible Travels

I did not screw up this title. Let me be perfectly clear. I do not mean *Gulliver's Travels* written by Jonathan Swift and I should not be confused with Lemuel Gulliver.

In order to fully distance myself from Swift's character, Gulliver, I want to recount some of the exotic travel that I have *not* experienced. I have never voyaged to Lilliput. I have not been shipwrecked. I have yet to swim for my life. I have never been taken prisoner. Brobdingnag does not yet have a church, so my denomination has never sent me there.

My ministry job does, however, afford me the opportunity to do some Gulliver-like travel. I have trekked through many stormy congregational business meetings but have not been blown off-course. I have been converged upon in rest rooms, parking lots, and hallways yet never actually seized by natives. Laputa is not hostile to denominational leadership. I have never been captured by pirates—the Pittsburgh variety or otherwise. Having noted all of this, I have heard through the unofficial church grapevine that Luggnagg is being considered for a church plant by a radical sect with highly communal tendencies. Maybe some day I'll get there. Church plants are paradise, you know.

At any rate, in spite of not being Gulliver, I have done some traveling. I have visited some interesting and strange places. I have seen a few Yahoos! And on occasion, I have been a pretty gullible explorer.

What follows are a couple of reflections from some of *my* Gullible Travels.

I was in a rush to get home. I had just spent the week at a bishop's and church executive's meeting at the edge of the Nation's Capitol. Speeding along the D.C. Beltway, I caught a glimpse of a humongous highway sign. HAZMAT was sprawled out in gigantic letters for all to see. (It was great to see that all hazardous materials were being identified, separated out, and forced into my lane!)

Instantly I thought, "Wow! What a great idea for the church. We should identify all of the cruddy stuff that keeps polluting, weakening, and killing the church—gossip, political maneuvering, selfish ambition, control issues, lifeless tradition—and separate them out, force them into one long pew, have a big truck come by, load them up, and take them to the Toxic-Church-Stuff Landfill.

Wouldn't that be great? By collecting and directing this hazardous material into one location, we could avert a disaster by containing contaminated bits and pieces from spreading throughout the church.

Another Gullible Travel occurred when I was driving through the countryside of Lancaster County, Pennsylvania. I came upon an unadorned roadside advertisement. On tattered cardboard appeared these handwritten, paint-scribbled words: *CORN / BEANS / TOMATOES / MELONS / HOMEMADE BREAD.* This homespun signage provided a Madison Avenue appeal for goodness. It simply sat there and shouted: *Fresh stuff. Home grown. Home baked.* I could smell it and taste it and I was still 300 yards away! This is good . . . right?

Absolutely, it is . . . well, at least *most* of the time. Yet ministry travels have taught me that "the good" is always less than "the essential." For instance, how often does "the good" steal attention from the necessary? Churches are notorious for this. Ripe issues steal focus. In-season pet projects pilfer attentiveness. Freshly baked programs (not to be confused with half-baked) constantly embezzle energy. All of this while the church routinely ignores the Spirit-placed signs for safe travel: Curve Ahead! Yield! Stop! Fines Doubled in Work Area! Only 10 miles to Paradise . . . Pennsylvania that is! Simply put, the good is not always the best.

The leader's journey is a distraction-laden excursion. Trading a beans-and-bread focus for a sharp-curve-ahead warning is ludicrous. Yet, there are times when we do it. We so focus in on the good, we neglect the grand. We exchange the "right" parking lot plan, "proper" hymnal, or "to-die-for" sound system, for healthy relationships. We savor the advertised produce and miss the defining turn.

Gullible Travels keep me focusing on the essentials.

### The Leader's Prayer:

God of Best Things . . . keep me paying attention. Give me a hand with watching the signs of the day. Teach me what is hazardous, what is "good" but not best, and what is yours and not mine. Protect this gullible leader as I seek to travel with you. In the name of the One who taught us to be as wise as serpents, and as harmless as doves . . . Amen.

# A Mother's Ears

Not long ago I was reintroduced to *Mother's Ears*—those marvelous hearing devices that fathers don't seem to possess. These auditory wonders hear all kinds of significant sounds in the night, like a half-wakened toddler's faint call "to go potty" or a frightened tot's soft whimper induced by a yucky dream. Victoria, my wife, seems to still have her original set of *Mother's Ears*, and they appear to be in great working order! These trademark ears immediately pick up on sounds like "Grandma, can I have a drink of water?" Or "Grandma, I dropped my blankie." Or "Grandma, can I get up now?" Many men seem to be void of these God-endowed auditory miracles. Let me illustrate. Somehow, peculiarly preoccupied by the rigors of work or the prevailing presence of ESPN, I *occasionally* miss an important message or two! It is at that very moment that *Mother's Ears* are mystically transformed into the *Wife's Voice*, and I become fully mindful that I've missed something I needed to hear.

Could it be that we, as church leaders, need to be reintroduced to a first-class set of *Mother's Ears* or the perceptive power of a *Wife's Voice*? Could it be that we need to perk up and listen to all the significant calls and whispers around us? In these difficult postmodern church times of waning vitality, cheapened commitment, declining worship attendance, and dwindling fiscal resources, could it be that the church and its leaders need to hear a soft distant voice calling out truth in the night? Maybe so. Maybe we need to sit up in bed, drop the channel changer, and truly listen with *Mother's Ears*.

Sadhu Sundar Singh, the Indian Christian mystic, utters a distant word into the night of the western church. This word breaks into our preoccupation with an *enlightened* culture and pricks the heart and soul of all who can hear. Sundar (1889-1929) penned this commentary:

"Once when I was in the Himalayas, I was sitting upon the bank of a river; I drew  out of the water a beautiful, hard, round stone and I smashed it. The inside was quite dry. The stone had been lying a long time in the water, but the water had not penetrated the stone. It is just like that with 'Christian' people of the West. They have for centuries been surrounded by Christianity, entirely steeped in its blessings, but the Master's truth has not penetrated them. Christianity is not at fault; the reason lies rather in the hardness of their hearts. Materialism and intellectualism have made their hearts hard. So I am not surprised that many people in the West do not understand what Christianity really is." (Reprinted from www.bruderhof.com. Copyright 2003 by The Bruderhof Foundation, Inc. Used with permission.) If these words bear any semblance of truth for the early1900s, then they are a hushed wail in the night of today's American church. May leaders who have a *Mother's Ear* to hear, hear what the Spirit whispers in the night. May we tune in to this gentle voice of the Spirit's call.

### The Leader's Prayer:

God who calls out in the night . . . call to your church again. Give us, your leaders, ears that are able and willing to hear. Tune me in. Let me hear your voice, your calls, and the pleadings of your people. As your agent in this day and age, help me to pay attention more intently and respond more graciously. May the affectionate tone of your voice stir me to action. In the name of your Son—the best listener of all . . . Amen.

# Resurrection People

Peter and John sped toward Jesus' tomb. Scripture doesn't record which ran faster . . . their feet or their mind. Both body and mind must have felt like they were running a hundred miles an hour! Mary had just told them that the stone—the huge weighty barrier that had crushed all their dreams—had been taken away.

These coarse fishermen were shocked! Staggered! Bewildered! What could have happened? Minds spinning. Feet running. Speculation whirling. Fear surging. Panting for both breath and life, they approached the tomb and sneaked a peek into the cave. Each one entered this empty space filled with a perplexing hope. Each sketched a conclusion in his own heart.

Mary trailed behind the men in this wild race back to the tomb. Nevertheless, she too must have dashed back at break-neck speed. Arriving on the scene, she paused, stepped back, and wept. Her eyes were filled with tears. Her mind filled with confusion. Her heart filled with a befuddled grief—a strange and unsettled feeling that she couldn't explain and that she couldn't shake. Through the tears, she stooped down to peek into what would become the empty space of her destiny. What ensued was beyond her wildest imagination. She chatted with angels. She unwittingly conversed with Jesus without even recognizing him.

Suddenly an amazing thing transpired. Jesus called her by name. "Mary." What a sound! The voice. His voice! Her mind raced. Her heart pounded. "It's him. It's him! It's Jesus." She knew it! He wasn't dead. He was alive! He was REALLY alive! The sound of his voice speaking her name melted her heart, opened her eyes, and turned her tears of grief to gushing joy. And, Mary became first among the new Resurrection People.

Wow! What a great story! What power and majesty and might and unbridled awe consumed Mary's heart. But what about the others? What about Peter and John and all the other disciples? How would they respond to the living Jesus? When he came and actually stood among them, would they be any less overwhelmed than Mary? Absolutely not! Resurrection People—resurrection leaders of every age—are continuously mesmerized by God's breathtaking Easter power—enthralled with wonder, splendor, and a holy bewilderment.

While much of the institutional church wrangles over budgets, flowers, building projects, choir seating, carpet color, padding pews, staff employment, sermon length, pastoral imperfections, worship styles, music preference, candle light at Communion, or the planting of memorial vegetation, Jesus still calls his leaders by name and waits to see if they will recognize his voice. He continues to defy death and show up in unexpected places. He stands among us and waits to see if anyone will notice.

Resurrection People, Resurrection Leaders, and Resurrection Churches endlessly revel in this wow-filled triumph of God. Can you hear him calling your name?

## The Leader's Prayer:

Voice of the Empty Tomb . . . keep calling my name. Call it loudly. Call it clearly. Call it out that I might unmistakably know that it's really you. Keep calling me to your side . . . to your life . . . to your surprise . . . to your work. Allow me to run in the grand Easter Derby alongside Peter and John and Mary. At the tomb's finish line, may I find you gone; out of the clench of death and into the grasp of grace. As your leader, may I always distinguish the sound of your voice. In the name of the One who calls my name . . . Amen.

# What Works?

What works? I hear this *all* the time. This ant-sized inquiry is a common topic for church boards. This pigmy probe is echoed equally in formal and casual conversations among every variety of church leadership. This little giant of a phrase is elevated by parachurch organizations. These two words are pitched in nearly every professional ministry journal headline or advertisement at one time or another. Name-recognized "super pastors" franchise it. Religious publishing houses propagate it. Christian bookstores dispense it. Everybody seems to want to know, "What works?"

The phraseology "What works?" by and large includes all sister-like phrases: How is that working for you? Is it working with the traditional folks? Does it work for youth? Will it work in a small country church? Can it work at the contemporary worship service? What will work for senior adults? Does it really work?

If it does work, will my church embrace it? At this point, please feel free to add your own favorite attention-grabbing phrase. No matter the phraseology, as leaders, we seem to have an insatiable appetite for *what works*!

I'm not 100% certain of every potential meaning for *what works*, but I do have a number of observations concerning several of the implications. *What works* gives the impression of seizing the prevailing *church thing*—the latest and most fashionable spiritual mania to "save the church," the pious program that will usher in a new era of church growth, or the sacred slant that will provide a dash of angelic zip to worship without driving away those who think that any form of zippy is an anathema! *What works* is far too often merely the language of the hot and holy quick fix . . . the corporate church version of accomplishment . . . the how-to manual for church achievement . . . or *The Ministry Guide to Success for Dummies*!

Now, before I am blindfolded and executed by the Success Patrol, let me confess my own desire for wanting to know what really works. Who among us does not want to know what will make our ministry more effective and efficient? Who in their right ministry mind doesn't want to have some bona fide Kingdom success? After all, Jesus didn't send his servants out into the world and instruct them to fail! He wanted them (and us) to succeed. So, after years of church-watching, and at the risk of sounding way (and I do mean *way!*) too simplistic, here is my observation of what *really* works:

- Worship that is authentic, lively, and God-impassioned.

- Vision that sets the tone, the atmosphere, and the purpose for ministry.

- People who know they are spiritually gifted, congregationally empowered, and fully released for mission-minded ministry.

- Leaders who are Christ-centered, tradition-honoring and seeker-conscious.

- Grounded leaders with a tough hide and tender heart.

- Leaders who sense *a call* from God to keep tending the flock even when the sheep really stink.

- Prayer that exhibits a clearly noticeable personal relationship with God.

- Preaching that is Scripture-focused and authoritative without being authoritarian.

It may sound way too simple. It may *be* too simple. But I've watched it. And it really seems to be *what works*!

### The Leader's Prayer:

Lord of What Works . . . take me to a new place. Take me past the ministry fads, the chic programs, and the well-dressed curriculum of today. Take me beyond the fashionable drawing cards, the designer missions, and the vogue worship experiences. Take me to someplace real and alive and filled with your presence. Take me further than I have ever been before. Take me—clueless, afraid, kicking, and screaming—to that place where I know what *really* works for you. In the name of Jesus, the One who forever knows what really works . . . Amen.

# *Falling Stars*

Scientists tell us that falling stars are small solid bodies which enter the Earth's atmosphere as they travel through space. These stars are commonly called meteors.

Meteors can plunge into the atmosphere at velocities ranging from ten to seventy kilometers per second. Consequently, the friction that is created is great enough to cause the meteor to begin burning up. This produces the light that we refer to as a falling star.

As a kid growing up in Indiana (one of the most geographically monotonous states in the Union) I was fascinated with falling stars. A night time spotting among buddies produced an instant reaction, "Look! Look! Look over there. There it goes! Did you see it? Did you see it? Look!" A collective "Wow!" echoed through the whole gang. To a bunch of country kids on a summer's night, falling stars were cool.

Years later I would learn about another kind of falling star. These stars aren't as brilliant as the ones shooting across a clear northern Indiana night sky; far too often, they're not glorious at all. This variety can be found anywhere—in your home town, in your school, in your place of employment, in your church, and even in your family. These luminaries can be found all the way from the White House, to the court house, to the church house. These stars are frequently persons we look up to, admire, and aspire to emulate. For me, they were the baseball heroes of my youth–Mickey Mantle, Stan Musial, Ernie Banks, Roberto Clemente, Hank Aaron, Willy McCovey, Willie Mays, and Bob Gibson. In the eyes of a small-town boy from Indiana, these were some of my grandest and shimmering stars—baseball meteors.

Somewhere along the way, I began to recognize that stars—both the heavenly and the earthly variety—have a certain staying power and possess creative qualities which impact multiple generations of witnesses. But falling stars are different. Falling stars flash brightly, make a grand celestial splash, and streak speedily out of sight. The brilliance fades. The light blackens. The glory dies. It's there. Then in an instant, it's gone!

While I know that there is a scientific explanation for this occurrence among heavenly bodies, I am more familiar with the human variety. Pride can burn them up. Chasing success can compromise their appointed luster. Jealousy can consume their brilliance. Steroids can tarnish their radiance. Immorality can taint their glory.

Deceptive behavior can eclipse their glimmer. And their shocking fall splashed across the evening news can break a little boy's heart.

As leaders in the church, there are those who look up to us, admire us, and even seek to emulate us. While we may not view ourselves as *spiritual meteors*, there are those who look up and see us as an exceptional light.

My grandson, Topher, was recently discovered standing behind a short table jabbering away. Gesturing from left to right, he was yakking up a storm. When quizzed about what in the world he was doing, in his best southern drawl, he declared, "I'm preachin'!" In actuality, he was reflecting and mimicking the illumination seen in his daddy.

Church leaders are called to a favored place. So shine! Blaze with God's glory. Keep your fire. Keep your radiance. Keep the glow of your joy. Keep your focus and integrity. Keep being the God-honoring person you were appointed to be. And finally, keep the role of church leader filled with wow and wonder; be a shining example that little boys and little girls will look up to, admire, and seek to emulate.

Keep your *God-twinkle* and you will never be a falling star.

## The Leader's Prayer:

Creator of the stars . . . burn brightly. As you lit the night's sky and pathway for the wise men and shepherds, and as you still light the way for sojourners, pilgrims, explorers, and faith-travelers of every stripe; so Lord, continue to shine down your glory. Fill me with your radiance, sparkle all the way through me as a church leader, and help me to glow with your love, your grace, and your peace. In the name of the One who lights the way . . . Amen.

# *Fast Food for Thought*

Not long ago, I sat in an Alban Institute seminar and heard an astonishing statement. The consultant, an authority on evangelism and congregational outreach, was speaking about cultural trends and the changing landscape of religious life in America and around the world. During his presentation he remarked that for centuries the Cross—Christianity's symbol of sacrifice, love, salvation, and God's forgiveness and mercy in and through Jesus Christ—was the single most recognizable symbol in the entire world. However he was quick to point out that all of this has changed.

It seems the Cross had been knocked off the gold medal stand in the worldwide Olympics of Symbol Recognition. There is a new symbol . . . a new winner . . . a new Olympic champion! The Cross has now been awarded the silver medal. The gold medal goes to (strike up the national anthem) . . . the Golden Arches! Yes, that's right. Ray Kroc's fast-food love child, McDonald's, and its legendary Golden Arches, have replaced the Christian Cross as the world's most recognizable symbol. [Cited from Guinness World Records; also noted in *Fast Food Nation: The Dark Side of the All-American Meal* by Eric Schlosser, Harper Perennial, January, 2002.]

In some baffling but very real way, the promotion of Big Macs, Egg McMuffins, Happy Meals, McNuggets, and those tasty little fries—all scrumptiously located under the Golden Arches—has expanded its global identity beyond that of the Gospel of Christ. What a *McShame* on the church!

As church leaders ponder cultural trends in the changing landscape of American life, they would do well to consider sampling some of these McNuggets of Data:

☐ Eighty-five percent of parents with children under age thirteen believe they have primary responsibility for teaching their children about religious beliefs. However, the vast majority spend no time during a typical week sharing with their children concerning matters of faith. Only about two-thirds attend religious services at least once a month. Parents rely upon their church to do all of the religious training of their children. [Cited from John Mark Ministries at: http://jmm.aaa.net.au/articles/10935.htm.]

☐ A survey of 12,000 senior high students found that moral behavior of teens who claimed a strong faith in Christ was only *slightly* different than non-Christian teens. Among the Christian teens: 74% had cheated on a test; 83% had lied to a teacher; 93% had lied to a parent; 63% had used physical violence against another person; 80% claimed that *all truth is relative to the individual and his or her circumstances*; 72% believe that *you can tell if something is morally or ethically right for you by whether or not it works in your life.* ["It's Time for a Revolution in Youth Ministry" by Josh McDowell and Ron Luce. *Group*, May 6, 2003 (Vol 29, No 4). Pages 53-55.]

☐ "This generation is so hungry for something that is authentic, and they're hungry for community. They have a great cheese-o-meter. They can smell if you're a hypocrite or a fake right away." [Dan Burgoyne, founder of *707*, a new worship ministry, quoted in *Baptists Today*, June 2003. Page 6.]

So, what does the modern *McChurch* have to serve up to this religiously hungry generation? How can we feed this drive-thru cohort without theologically dumbing down spiritual core values and serving up *Dollar Menu* holiness? Will supersized programs and theme-driven facilities deliver authentic intimacy with God? Can *Happy Meal* faith (get the Joseph and Mary bobble-head collectables while they last) sustain those caught in the chilly gusts of day-to-day living?

Given these facts about the Cross, and that increasing numbers of people now seem to embrace the Golden Arches above the Golden Rule; what will we, as leaders, do to promote the lip-smacking-*good-news* message of God's love and mercy in Christ Jesus?

This fast food for thought is ready for take out!

## *The Leader's Prayer:*

God of Golden Streets and Golden Truth . . . give me wisdom. Give me a wisdom that is not my own but that which comes from above—that which is squarely yours. Show me how to reach out with meaning and purpose and nourishment to this hungry generation of spiritual consumers. Enlarge the *Good News Menu* of ministry. Help me grab the attention of those with an appetite for more. In the name of the One who is food for my soul and object of the disciples' creative *Taste and See* promotion . . . Amen.

# The Wonderful Church

A number of years ago, when I was still in the pastorate, a woman approached me following one of our membership classes. She walked right up to me and, with a twinkle in her eyes, proclaimed, "This is a wonderful church. Do you know what you have here?" It must have been a rhetorical question, because she quickly gasped for breath and enthusiastically told me exactly what we had going for us. Wow! What a great feeling for a pastor. I was elated that our church was so wonderful . . . even if not everybody was equally thrilled.

Through the years, I have mulled over this brief episode in my church life. It has caused me to reflect on the *Wonderful Church* concept. By this I don't mean identifying all of the programs or ministries that make for a wonderful church. I'm quite certain that there are as many views on this topic as there are church members with a voice box and an opinion. What impacts me in all of this is the word *wonderful*. I love to play with words. So, please permit me to explore a small bit of wordplay on the gist and virtue of the term *wonderful*. Consider these: Wonder-full. Wonder-filled. Wonder-packed. Wonder-crammed. Wonder-complete. Wonder-satisfied. Wonder-occupied. Wonder-engaged. Wonder-jammed. Wonder-plump.

The above word musings add up to what I call *Church Wonderment*. Church Wonderment is that marvelous, miraculous, phenomenal sense of sacred awareness mingled with a lavish splash of holy curiosity. The result: a God-is-present awe, Revelation-Four-like worship, and shouts of, "Holy, Holy, Holy!"

This kind of Church Wonderment elicits an Isaiah 6 "Here am I! Send me." proclamation. This brand of Church Wonderment provokes an Ephesians 1 declaration, "For he has made known to us in all wisdom and insight the mystery of his will, according to his purpose which he set forth in Christ as a plan for the fullness of time . . . [and now] we who first hoped in Christ have been destined and appointed to live for the praise of his glory." (Ephesians 1:9-10, 12 RSV).

This strain of Church Wonderment casts aside all restraints, grabs a pricey flask of alabaster, rushes to the feet of Jesus, wets his feet with tears, wipes them with hair, kisses them, and anoints them with the balm of a woman's sacrificial love and devotion. Holy Wonderment! What a church that would be!

So, where is it? Where is the Wonderful (Wonder-full / Wonder-filled / Wonder-jammed / and, don't forget Wonder-plump!) church of today?

As leaders, we know that far too often the church of today is Wonder-empty. The God-awe has been stripped away, labeled as "emotionalism," and ordered out of town. Holy curiosity has been "intellectualized" and matter-of-factly explained away. The marvelous has been "downgraded" to the customary and casually brushed aside. The miraculous has been "demythologized" and subsequently dismissed as ancient story rhetoric. The phenomenal has been marked "discontinued" and considered no longer available. Wonder-full has become Wonder-empty.

As a result, the Wonderful Church of Jesus frequently sits nearly empty. And sadly, our only wonder is about why.

### The Leader's Prayer:

God of Wonder . . . fill me once more with the marvel of your love, your mercy, your grace, your joy, your peace, and your creation. Infuse my life and my church with a grand display of your presence. Forgive us, as leaders, for downplaying your glory. Restore the ALL of your splendor. In the precious name of your Wonder-filled Son . . . Amen.

# Mystified

I am over and over again mystified (I mean seriously baffled) by some of the perspectives I hear being put forth in our common congregational journey. See if any of these goings-on rings true to your experience. If so, let's debunk these church-life foibles.

The <u>Mystification</u>: "I love the early worship service. I get to go to church; and then, I can get on with the rest of my day," piped a woman in her critique of the congregation's newly created worship service.

The <u>Debunking</u>: The highest calling of God in attending an early worship service is not to show up, punch your *I-Went-to-Church* ticket, and beat the Methodists and Presbyterians to the all-you-can-eat buffet. The highest calling of God in worship is to be in his presence, experience the wonder of his majesty, drink in the life-sustaining substance of his Word, and be personally restored.

The <u>Mystification</u>: "I hate those *little ditties*!" This is the angry proclamation of Mabel, an unhappy camper who wants her congregation to have nothing to do with singing those mindless petty choruses that have invaded her worship space.

The <u>Debunking</u>: Frankly, it never ceases to amaze me when I hear some folks condemn all choruses as *little ditties*—or their derogatory endearment of choice; and yet, those same folks seem perfectly content to sing a "good old hymn" that originated as a bar room tune. Who'd a thunk it?

The <u>Mystification</u>: "This is *my* church. I've been here all my life. This pastor won't be here forever. I can wait her out!" This was Bob's hostile outcry at the congregation's latest celebration of Grumble Fest.

The <u>Debunking</u>: I can't help but speculate at Bob's surprise when Jesus reveals to him that it is not actually "Bob's church" but *his*. And, as for the unwanted pastor, she was there at *his* invitation.

The <u>Mystification</u>: We were gathered for the first meeting of the Pastoral Search Committee. I asked the members to please introduce themselves and give a brief statement or two about why they were selected for the committee. One by one they shared. It was Mary's introduction that mystified me. She began, "My name is Mary. I sit in the third pew on the left, the second seat in." I didn't hear another word. I could only think, "Wow! What if we bring a pastor in here, the church grows, and somebody sits in her pew!"

The <u>Debunking</u>: If you really want the church to grow (one of the recurrent claims of most pastoral search committees), you may need to scoot over.

The <u>Mystification</u>: Another Search Committee dandy happened this way. As the pastoral candidate was being interviewed and shared about how his previous church had grown—both attendance and membership had increased significantly—the youngest member of the Search Committee interrupted, "If you come to our church, you won't do that [grow the church] will you? I like our church just the way it is." As a professional, I have been trained to never show shock; but this one almost had me!

The <u>Debunking</u>: How is the Kingdom of God expected to increase if the local church is not willing to grow?

There is a dreadful amount of puzzling thinking in today's churches. Unless we, as leaders, are willing to embark on a candid debunking campaign, I fear that many congregations will remain befuddled with emotion, perplexed by bursts of self-absorption, bamboozled with confusing theology, and at a total loss to comprehend what in the world has happened to *their* church. In a phrase, they'll remain mystified!

## *The Leader's Prayer:*

God of Understanding and Enlightenment . . . show yourself. Break into each Kingdom-harmful attitude. Shatter the *it's-all-about-me* mindset. Smash the congregational *I-Cycle* in which we seem to spin. And then, grant your leaders the insight and the courage to move your church to a new day . . . to a new place . . . to a new way of thinking . . . to a fresh way of being church together. In this way, our grandest mystery will be in you alone. In the name of the One who scooted off his throne for us . . . Amen.

# Pennsylvania Driving

Not long after we moved to Pennsylvania, I was driving home from a church meeting in southern Lancaster County. I sped along with a thousand things dashing through my mind. Then it hit me; I was headed east and home was west. Home was directly behind me! Panic attack. I was literally racing away from my goal as fast as I could go.

The bizarre point is this: I was on the right road. I was going the right direction. I remember thinking, *this is nuts!* Then I had one of those weird, ever-increasing *remember-you're-driving-in-Pennsylvania-now* moments. Hello. Direction alert! Remember Craig, this is the wonderful Keystone state. You're not in Indiana any more. [I grew up in Indiana where roads run straight. If you are traveling north in the Hoosier State and turn right, it is *always* east!] You're in Pennsylvania and sometimes you have to go east to get west. Pennsylvania driving means that on occasion home has to be behind you before it can be in front of you.

What a great life-lesson! From time to time leaders must learn to go east to get west. They need to know traveling a few miles north to head south is okay. It does well for those who labor in ministry to pause and remember the context of our ministry, the background of our culture, and the topography of our congregational landscape. While we drive the back roads of church growth, community outreach, and global awareness; while we speed toward multiple worship services, sparking capital campaigns, and mobilizing laity; while we explore contemporary music, building a new facility, and a unified mission statement, we need to be reminded that home may actually need to be behind us before it can be in front of us. Failure to consider this perspective may cause us to mistake common side roads for damaging detours.

Consider Joseph who was told to take Mary and Jesus and flee to Egypt (see Matthew 2:13). This is a strange direction if this child is to be at home and "save his people from their sins." (Matthew 1:21). Yet down the road apiece, Joseph is instructed to "Rise, take the child and his mother, and go to the land of Israel." (Matthew 2:20). So, was Joseph on a wild goose chase in the desert? Did he pursue a damaging detour, or was his directional escapade a divine direction? Hopefully, we all know the answer.

Consider Derrick, an influential deacon who led the charge against hiring a new youth pastor. A church business meeting was called to vote on whether or not the church should employ its first-ever youth pastor. When the voice vote was taken, he shouted at the top of his lungs, "No!" Regrettably, the moderator of the meeting tallied the verdict based on *volume* rather than *vote*. The vote failed. Yet two years down the pike, Derrick turned a corner, went a whole new direction, changed his tune, and his 180-degree motion led the charge to call for our very first youth pastor. So, was this a damaging detour? Some would say so. Or, was this divine direction? I believe the latter!

Having encountered my fair share of these discombobulating side trips, I offer these simple Pennsylvania-driving thoughts for your *Tour-de-Nuts* through ministry:

- Never lose sight of home.

- Just because home is behind you doesn't mean you are headed in the wrong direction.

- If you are sure of the way, don't let skeptics dissuade you.

- It pays to learn your congregational countryside.

- Remember, not every twist and turn is a damaging detour.

*The Leader's Prayer:*

Creator of Winding Roads . . . keep me between the lines and always headed in your direction. Post signs and signals so I will never be off your beaten path. Forgive me when I fancy fast thoroughfares and wide, straight boulevards but you send me down narrow side streets or curvy country roads. Simply direct me. Help me understand that it is not about east or west but about you, your destination, and your arrival time. In the name of the One whose journey forever leads back to you . . . Amen.

# The Worship Ordeal

After all these years of so called Worship Wars—the ongoing clash between *contemporary* worshippers and *traditional* worshippers—one of the long drawn out questions among a number of medium-sized congregations continues to be: "Should we begin a second worship service?" This is a painstaking query with scores of opinionated members ready, willing, and able to line up and make their notorious *This Is What We Need To Do* speech. As usual, many of these speeches have been well prepared and rehearsed long before any facts have actually been presented.

Okay, sarcasm aside, it is fair to say that this topic does generate a remarkable amount of controversy. It's like trying to get an American President elected with more than a 51% margin—red pew worshippers to one side and blue pew worshippers to the other.

All in all, there are a number of very good reasons for beginning a second worship service. There are also more than a few very bad reasons. In my consulting with congregations, I have experienced some of both. Good leaders need to be prepared to assist the congregation with this decision fully aware that they may well get verbally blasted from both red and blue sides.

Below are ten reasons to start a second worship service. Five reasons are compelling. Five reasons are appalling. Please read on and check your score against the *Worship-Ordeal-O-Meter*:

Reason One: Everybody else is doing it.

Reason Two: A church consultant—who doesn't know a lick about our church culture—told us to do it.

Reason Three: It is a part of the Congregational Master Plan to promote unity through the strategic separation of warring musical factions.

Reason Four: To energize our church life by providing a contemporary worship format for singing a rousing chorus of "Kumbaya."

Reason Five: So the Church Board Chair's daughter will have a chance to play her base guitar and the Head Deacon's twelve-year-old son can fool around with his drums.

Reason Six: To reach unchurched persons with a new style of worship with the hope of introducing (or reintroducing) them to Christ.

Reason Seven: To infuse a spark of modern-day worship vitality back into a declining or stale congregational life cycle.

Reason Eight: To take action; to launch something fresh without eliminating existing services or the healthy role of tradition.

Reason Nine: New worship services commonly attract or keep persons with a different longing for worship or music.

Reason Ten: An additional service can often serve as a vehicle to reconnect inactive members who may be ready to come back and try again.

Well, how did you do? If you identified numbers 1-5 as somewhat appalling and numbers 6-10 as somewhat compelling, you win!

In the end, if you are going to start a second worship service, take the necessary time to do your homework and planning. Have a specific purpose, a target group, or a compelling motive. Expect to hear a few words from gloomy Gus and murky Mary. Get congregational support for the vision and, of course, pray.

When all is said and done, do it for God's glory and compelling reasons.

### *The Leader's Prayer:*

God of Tradition and Change . . . lean on us; press us! Compel your people to put down the weapons of harsh words, musical politics, and rigid territorialism. Open our minds, hearts, and doors to *all* who would come to worship you. Keep traditions faithful. Keep methods pliable. Keep moving us forward. Lead me, as I seek to lead others, in this central piece of our life together. In the name of the One who embodied faithful tradition and faith-filled change . . . Amen.

# Random Musing

Please stick with me in this chapter. I want to toss out three very different thoughts. They may appear as hit and miss senseless ramblings. Maybe they are, but hang in there. From time to time I find that disjointed thinking can be an art form!

*Random Thought Number One*: On my way to Pottstown, Pennsylvania, I zipped through McDonald's at the Morgantown Exit off of the PA Turnpike. (A double cheeseburger and fries periodically soothes the weary soul of a famished and hurried church leader.) As I juggled my McGoodies and maneuvered my little red Honda toward the highway, I saw "it." Right there in front of me, right before my eyes in GIANT letters  no one could miss: HIRING - APPLY NOW - $7.50 TO START. McDonald's was hiring!

McDonald's hiring isn't ordinarily exciting news, but this hadn't been a good week. Sooo . . . my escapist thinking took over. "Hey, ministry isn't everything. What about Burger-flipping? It can't be all that bad. Cheeseburgers don't form committees! Fries don't fight over what kind of fat they're going to be cooked in! Happy Meals don't fuss over the color of their bag! There is no public dipping sauce controversy!" This could be good! (It really was a bad week!) But just as rapidly as this run-away thinking dashed into my head, my thoughts shifted back to ministry. Almost instantly revelation struck. I was back!

Check this out. What if we could finance ministry by McTithing? It may sound really weird but don't turn your nose up at it until you crunch all the numbers.

Consider this: $7.50 per hour for 40 hours equals $300 per week. A tithe (10%) equals $30 per week. Multiplied by 100 weekly tithers, this equals $3,000 per Sunday. Multiply this by 52 Sundays and you get $156,000!! McWow! And what would happen if some of these folks got overtime? What if a couple of them were shift managers? How about one store manager? One district manager? One owner?

Financing the Kingdom is always supersized when tithing is a part of our regular order. Remember, when faith infuses the simplest of giving, the dollars will take care of themselves.

*Random Thought Number Two*: Over the years I have become increasingly aware of the persecution of fellow believers around the world. On a trip to Nigeria several years ago, I heard Rev.

Toma Ragnjiya—then President of the Church of the Brethren in Nigeria and still a dear friend—quote Tertullian with these words, "The blood of the martyrs is the seed of the church."

With escalating tension between Muslims and Christians around the world, with atheistic affronts to Christian faith here at home, with watered down versions of spirituality abounding, where does your church stand? A strange picture in the American church culture is coming into full view. It seems, while countless numbers of believers around the world risk shedding their own blood for their faith, the American church rarely breaks a sweat.

How is your church at risk-taking? If the answer is, "Not so good," then push back the boundaries of your Holy Comfort Zone. If nothing else, you will be taking a risk yourself and setting the example for a perspiration-less Body of Christ.

*Random Thought Number Three*: Loneliness is rampant among church leaders. Living in glass houses, yet strangely isolated, far too many church leaders feel very much alone. For this reason, jump in and be a part of the solution. Take a minute to call and encourage a ministry partner. Jot a note of support to a Kingdom colleague. Email a verbal hug to a spiritual coworker. If *you* don't understand the nuances and isolation in ministry, there is a very good chance *no one* will. Collegial support and care is a great way to keep all of us healthy. (While this dynamic is at epidemic levels among pastors and professional church leaders, it is none the less valid for Christian leaders in the work place and in professional life.)

If *McTithing*—the minimum wage of fiscal faithfulness—can make a simple difference in supporting ministry, if risking a bead of sweat for Kingdom business can begin to move us from self-satisfaction to self-sacrificing, if a modest dose of encouragement administered to a ministry teammate can keep them in the game, then do it! Lead the way. Take initiative to be the leader God has called you to be.

## The Leader's Prayer:

Ruler of Holy Pandemonium and Wild Thoughts . . . expand my thinking. Fill me with creative and out-of-this-world views. Help me to discover new approaches, to risk more of myself, and to raise the spirits of those who minister alongside me. In the creative, risk-taking, and encouraging name of Jesus . . . Amen.

# *Appreciation*

Do you ever get gifts—those tangible signs of appreciation, endearment, or simple thanks for your leadership? I'm not certain about your church traditions or experiences in this regard, but for many congregations, Christmas seems to be the universal gift-giving season.

While pastoring in Orlando, Florida, I attended the area clergy association meeting. After running a powerful advertising campaign, I was elected vice-president. (Actually, I was the newest clergy in town and possessed a great inability to say no. This combination generally leads to some sort of church office!)

Not long after my call to serve the association, I joined the new president—a Greek Orthodox priest—and pastoral colleagues from the Church of the Nazarene, Church of God, Southern

Baptist Church, Presbyterian Church USA, and the United Methodist Church on a planning committee for a city-wide event. The group gathered for lunch at a local Greek restaurant owned by one of the priest's parishioners. We were treated like royalty! As we conveyed appreciation to our host clergy for the copious blessings which had been afforded us, we somehow wandered into a conversation about congregational expressions of appreciation. This is where the story takes an interesting twist.

The Greek Orthodox priest pulled a long, dark brown cigar from the inside pocket of his vestments, lit up, sat back, and began to tell about the Holy Land trip his congregation had surprised him with two Christmases ago. The Southern Baptist chimed in with his account of a memorable Christmas gift—an all expenses paid week-long cruise to the Caribbean. The Church of God (Cleveland, Tennessee – Pentecostal variety) preacher leaped in with an account of his congregation's Sunday morning shocker presentation—a set of car keys to a new Lincoln Town Car! The Presbyterian gave a brief word about a reasonable monetary gift and then sat in stoic silence. The United Methodist looked uneasy and fiddled with his water glass. The Nazarene gazed out the window. And me, well, I joked about the one-pound yuletide fruitcake that I found sitting on my desk! (I must confess. There was a part of me that wanted to be *Bapticostal* with a smattering of priestly Greek Orthodoxy!)

I'm not sure how your congregation chooses (or doesn't choose) to express appreciation to its leaders, but my great hope is that the curse of the annual yuletide fruitcake will be forever broken!

Nevertheless, no matter what the expression of appreciation or lack thereof, I want to assure you that quality leaders are appreciated by those who know the *real* challenges, frustrations, hurts, and discouragements that you (and your family) often face. May the One who sees in secret and knows your sacrificial efforts in ministry remember you with abundant gifts of grace, peace, joy, and close bonds with family and friends. May God's pleasure be mingled with the expressed gratitude of others to bring you encouragement and support in all seasons.

Finally, if you get a fruitcake and like it, great! If not, smile, use it as a doorstop! Remember: fruit, nuts, and a hearty belly-laugh will do you untold good.

## *The Leader's Prayer:*

God of Precious Gifts . . . bless each leader—pastors, deacons, board members, elders, and co-workers in Kingdom business—who are reading this book. Encourage them. Lift them up. Inspire them. Reward them with the intimate assurance of your incredible presence. Remind us all that trips are short, cruises come to an end, Town Cars rust, but the gift of your love endures forever and ever. In the name of the One who is the sweetest gift of all . . . Amen.

# *Lookin' Good!*

On a recent shopping trip, my wife, Victoria, bought me a new shirt. It's a summer tropical style—a don't-tuck-it-in-but-let-it-all-hang-out-and-chill-a-bit casual shirt—made by *Paradise Coves*. And it radiates with color. It is a deep dazzling turquoise! She says that I am a natural "winter" and this icy shade of turquoise is a great color for me. Well, it must be true, because when I put it on, she gave me her "you're lookin' good" smile. Inspired by her impish grin and robed in my brilliant 70% silk, 30% cotton, made in China armor, I went forth from my castle to slay the dragons of the day. After all, I was lookin' good!

But it didn't take long to remind Sir Turquoise that he was not invincible. Early that morning, before donning the dynamic threads of victory, I had popped in my contacts, downed my blood pressure medication, taken my morning dose of Glucosamine, rubbed my arthritic knee with a healthy dose of eucalyptus oil, strapped on my knee brace, and hobbled to the kitchen to pour myself a cup of coffee.

In the course of the day's activity, someone did comment on what a good color my shirt was for me. Her exact words were, "Hey, Craig. That's a great color for you." Apparently, I was still lookin' good. Yet underneath it all, I was tired, broken, and aching. The outside was lookin' good. But the inside, where no one could see, was falling apart.

In that moment, the Lord spoke to my heart about how true this is for many of us as church leaders. Sometimes—not all the time, but sometimes—our armor has us lookin' good. We slip on a lightly starched and freshly pressed shirt, carefully knot an unpretentious but cultured tie, don a new three-button suit, fasten on a Sunday morning smile, and go out to face the dragons of the day. (Attire and fashion ensemble will vary for women.) Beneath it all, however, we are tired, broken, and aching.

The ones who focus on the brilliant armor of our exterior garments will never really see what is beneath. They will not know the pain of ministry. They will not absorb the bruises of so-called constructive criticism. They will not become weary of living in a glass house where words and actions are regularly scrutinized. They will not notice the cuts, scratches, scars, or open wounds incurred in church leadership. But underneath it all, *you* know. You know all too well.

Nevertheless, there is a balm in Gilead, an oil that flows, a Hand that touches, and a Physician who heals. There is a promise—a sweet eucalyptus for the soul. There is a Man who sees clearly beneath the distinguished armor of leadership. He notices the unseen. He understands what is beneath the surface. He is not repulsed by what is concealed. He looks me in the eyes and peers deep inside. He smiles warmly. He reaches out and touches the hidden aches and buried pains and secret wounds.

When he's finished, I am ready to strap on my knee brace, hobble to the kitchen, pour a cup of coffee, and do it *all* over again.

## The Leader's Prayer:

Lord Jesus . . . thank you. Thank you for bearing the load of leadership with me. Thank you for seeing all that lies beneath—frailty, injury, uncertainty—and continuing to use me as your servant leader. Day after day after day after day, may your anointing linger upon me. May the balm of your healing and the mere presence of your touch, stir me to action. In the name of the One who sees beneath the surface . . . Amen.

# Things to Remember

Age is sneaky. And it's getting sneakier all the time! I know because without even asking, I get charged the senior's price for coffee at Burger King. People in their thirties and early forties frequently call me "sir." I get "mature checking" at my local bank. I actually read information about the new Medicare Plan. My football-injured knee gets stiff when I sit too long. My doctor informs me I should begin to have a regular colonoscopy. And I know that AARP is not the sound of a hair-lipped dog. As some of you know, the list could go on.

Age reminds me that my diet is supposed to change. I am expected to ingest low fat, high protein, low carbohydrates, high fiber, low sodium, and minuscule amounts of sugar—approximately the amount a small ant can carry up Mount Fuji on a single trip.

The bottom line is this: I am to choke down more of the things I endure, and less of the things I enjoy!

Aging can also be a significant cause of memory loss. I recently read an article about "Memory Foods." These are the foods engineered to keep you alert, keep the body fit, keep the heart vigorous, and keep the metabolism running and the memory sharp. This is great. But I want it all! I want the best of both worlds. I want the healthy and the yummy. In this day and age, why can't someone, some sympathetic cerebral culinary (kind of like the Food Science Department at Purdue University meets Rachael Ray), come up with a way to do it all?

Here is what I mean. I crave Ginkgo Swirl Cookie Dough ice cream. I long for saturated-fat-less prime rib with starch-less garlic mashed potatoes, creamed corn, and a small salad with the *House Dressing*—a tasty blend of heart-healthy fish oil, crumbled Fiber One, and zero-calorie blue cheese. I envision an extra large deep dish Chicago-style everything-on-it-but-anchovies supreme pizza with an extra helping of antioxidants. I yearn for a half dozen Krispy Kreme donuts filled with rich folic-acid-cream and crowned with fat-burning icing. And where is a mouthwatering lip-smacking double fudge flaxseed cheesecake when you want one?

Oh well, I guess if I have to eat better to remember better, I'd better get at it. There are still a few things worth remembering. This is especially true for church leaders who want to remain healthy. In no particular order, here are a few things worthy of recall:

1. Don't set out to save the world at the expense of losing your family.

2. Honor your spouse. After God, she/he (not the ministry) is number one.

3. Decide ahead of time what you will do when the hurts in ministry come.

4. Keep a sense of humor.

5. Have friends outside the church.

6. Remind yourself regularly how truly blessed you are.

7. If you are a pastor and ever get a chance to buy a house during your ministry years, do it. It makes a great place for furniture and grandchildren when you retire.

8. God has never created a perfect church.

9. You are not the savior of everybody's issues.

10. Let your scars remind you of God's healing.

11. Grace is a good thing to extend . . . especially to yourself.

12. Say something good about Jesus every chance you get.

Finally, you should remember that most of ministry is exactly what you make of it. Oh, I almost forgot . . . eat some blueberries. Blueberries are rich in anthocyanins and help to keep blood vessels supple and transport nerve impulses more efficiently.

## *The Leader's Prayer:*

God of All Provision . . . you never fail. Bless your treasured name. You are my Provider. You care for me in this life and in the life to come. Lord, satisfy my appetite with an increasing desire for good things. Keep my body strong, my mind healthy, and my focus on you. Feed my soul with nourishment from your Word that I might grow to remember all of the life lessons you prepare for me. In the name of the One who never forgets his love for me . . . Amen.

# Vision Revisited

I confess. I am a strong proponent of vision for the church. It is a key word in my vocabulary. It rumbles out of my mouth like thunder before an early summer's rain. For years I've been beating this drum and hammering out the message that Christian churches have too little vision. We think too small. We get in-grown too quickly. We have turned into *mom-and-pop* shopkeepers in a Sam's Club generation. Now, before some of you get all bent out of shape, I am not saying that there is no longer a place for the small church. There is. But what I am saying is this: there is more to a ministry vision than hosting the annual Sauerkraut Festival, keeping pew pad pencils sharpened, checking on Mrs. Grousebottom's hang nail, or being the last one out the church door in order to switch off the lights.

Having confessed my vision-driven bent, I am forced to revisit the full concept of vision. I still believe most churches think too small, get in-grown too quickly, and are hyper-focused on the microscopic tasks that blur vision and blind them to larger ministry possibilities. I also realize vision by itself is not enough. Vision is not an ecclesiastical knight in shining amour riding into a besieged congregational village and slaying the dragons of despair.

Over and over again, we view vision as that mystical missing link which is "out there" in the great organizational beyond merely waiting to rescue us. It is a secluded reality perched slightly out of reach. But if we could reach it . . . if we could just get there . . . if we could beckon its powerful presence, we would become a better people, a better church, and more faithful disciples of Jesus. If we could somehow "get it," we would reap the reward of a new way of living, a new way of being, a new found unity, and a brand new identity that has eluded us for so long. If we could somehow miraculously "touch it," we would solve our problems, banish our struggles, and soar into a grand and glorious future.

This brand of vision—the institutional savior variety—is bogus and misleading. It leads congregations to see a paradisiacal future through a Lens Crafter pair of rose-tinted glasses. It frequently mirrors past images of success, and in so doing, memorializes the church golden age which is long dead but never buried. Neither alternative is healthy, nor represents godly vision.

Yes, vision is important . . . very important. Nevertheless, it is limited. Vision can chart a course, drive goals, and even rally support for a building project. However, vision is not *The Answer* to churches' woes. When we create vision statements, reorganize structures, create long-range goals, initiate a contemporary worship service, or launch a food bank with the full expectation that "this vision" will be the end-all to congregational infirmity, we often miss the point. We miss the compelling need for a community of believers to tussle with the true purpose of the church. We mistakenly seek to *do* something rather than *be* something. With this approach and outlook, we fall into the alluring vision-trap where vision masquerades as solution.

By revisiting this subject, I have come to realize vision is not the wonder-working commodity I once believed it to be. Vision is not the *savior* of the church. The church is not fundamentally about vision casting so that new people will be attracted to worship, flawless (Robert's Rules of Order) business meetings will be conducted, seamless vision statements suitable for framing will be crafted, or a broad array of social programming will be initiated. We are the Church of Jesus Christ! As such, our primary work is not about vision. Our work, first and foremost, is about relationships and the incredible business of transformation.

Real vision is getting a 20/20 glimpse of a transformed community. Real vision is spotting a Christ-directed people who live changed lives. Real vision is seeing what it will take to provide Gospel-inspired, power-filled, word-and-deed ministry to those who are yet-to-be-transformed.

## *The Leader's Prayer:*

Creator of Vision . . . open me up to your transforming power. Save me from simple answers, quick-fix solutions, clever and powerless resolutions, and anything that is permanently suitable for framing. Captivate me once more with your pulsating love and life-altering call to leadership. Call your people to meaningful relationships. Rally your people to transformation ministry. Send us your Spirit and on your way. In the name of the One who brought vision to life . . . Amen.

# Playing the Percentages

I love *March Madness*! For those who are seriously sports-challenged, *March Madness* is the delirium of frenzied pomp swirling around the NCAA Basketball Tournament each March. It is the place where established hard court legends—North Carolina, Duke, Kansas, Kentucky—meet the upstart giant slayers like Winthrop, George Mason, SE Louisiana, and Bradley. It is the place where coaches who make a seven-figure income, host their own TV shows, and do prime time commercials, compete against coaches who simply *have* an income and *watch* TV commercials! As they travel the Road to the Final Four, each of them is playing the percentages in hopes of laying claim to the title: National Champion.

Playing the percentages is an essential part of every basketball coach's success. The key substitution of a quick small guard to handle the ball against a pressing defense, the insertion of a defensive specialist to hold off a late rally, the entry of a three-point shooter to rack up some quick points, a 30-second timeout to quiet a thundering crowd, a trapping press to rattle the freshman point guard, an aggressive double team to shut down the leading scorer—these strategies are all playing percentages in the pursuit of success.

All of this started me thinking about playing the percentages in ministry. Some church leaders provide leadership to larger well-established congregations with a rich history, ample finances, multiple staff, sophisticated ministry programming, and elaborate facilities. Others labor in smaller much less known congregational venues where tradition is fraught with hardships, ministry programming is a constant struggle, facilities are in disrepair, and an aging parishioner base gives rise to fiscal limitations and short-range vision. And, there are still others who labor, pouring out heart and soul, in the never-ending toil to create something out of nothing.

Church leaders, no matter their ministerial lot in life, are playing the percentages of ministry. They are spiritual coaches in quest of the right decision, the right call, the right maneuver, the right way to posture their congregation for Kingdom success. I am not certain what all of the *right* calls might be, nor am I prepared to calculate the success rate for each potential action. However I have been around long enough to know some of the percentages you should be familiar with if you intend to be successful in ministry:

- There is a 100% chance you will say something or do something that will profoundly change someone's life.

- There is a 100% chance you will at some time and in some way screw up and need to apologize.

- There is a 100% chance you will not minister in the perfect church.

- There is a 100% chance you are not the perfect leader.

- There is a 100% chance ministry will bless you in ways you never imagined.

- There is a 100% chance you will encounter the ugly side of church life.

- There is a 100% chance you will *not* meet ALL of the expectations of ALL of the people in the pews.

- There is a 100% chance you will *not* meet ALL of your own expectations.

Playing these percentages will not gain you the title National Champion; but forming a ministry game plan around these numbers and pairing this plan with some God-honoring perseverance will certainly merit the title Faithful Servant. And in the Mad March of Ministry, that's not bad.

## *The Leader's Prayer:*

Ageless Coach . . . you are 100% faithful. Praise your holy name! Give me the heart of a spiritual champion. Grant me wisdom, strength, and courage to make the *right* calls. Grant me the humility and fortitude to confess when I have blown it. Grant me grit to keep going, strength to keep working, hope to keep praying, and guts to stay in the game. In the March Madness of Ministry, keep reminding me that the University of Jesus is never "on the bubble," never eliminated early, and never falls victim to an upset. Help me learn by heart the final scene: the crowd shakes the rafters with delirious shouts of victory; conquering cheers of success ascend on high; the nets of this life are cut down . . . we win! In *your* wonderful name, the victory is Yours and ours . . . So be it, Game Over!

# Where the Water Flows

There is a creek that flows across the back of the property in Columbus, Ohio where Victoria and I purchased our first home. It produces a steady but modest flow of water. Truthfully, I'm not sure if it is a small creek or a large brook. (I don't really know the difference.) But I do know that it made an incredible place to go, sit, and listen to rustling leaves, chirping birds, and the wondrous babble of fresh water rippling across the imbedded rocks.

As a person searching for meaning in life—exploring what it really meant to be a husband and father and grappling with my vocational direction—a seat beside this soothing water was a precious retreat. This spot provided just the right place to pray, to ponder, and to sort out life.

Where soothing water flows remains a precious place for me. At this stage in life, I find myself seated, not beside a creek or brook, but in church pews. The rustling is not leaves, but bulletins filled with an order of service, announcements, or a children's handout. The chirping is not gathered birds, but assembled worshipers, choirs, and musicians. The wondrous babble rippling forth is not creek water bathing nearby rocks, but the fresh flow of spoken prayer, preaching, and conversation cleansing the human spirit with encouragement, hope, and grace.

I long to sit in a place where Living Water flows—the sound of movement, life, joy, peace, praise, challenge, assurance, and the fresh flow of God's Holy Spirit. Where *this* water flows, God plants and grows his Church. Where *this* water flows, people come to know Jesus as Savior. Where *this* water flows, people transition from salvation to discipleship. Where *this* water flows, people grow in love, mercy, grace, obedience, holiness, boldness, humility, and service. Where *this* water flows, people learn about the real meaning of life. Where *this* water flows, life-roles are clear: people find purpose and meaning in life's vocation and calling. Where *this* water flows there is *still time*: the wonderful blessing of precious quiet moments to pray, to ponder, and to sort out life.

Several years after we moved from our first home, Victoria and I stopped by to ask the new owners if we could look around and reminisce a bit. They graciously invited us in. As a part of this nostalgic mini-tour, I eventually made my way to the back yard, sauntered to the rear of the property, and was reacquainted with the old creek that meandered there. Tears rolled down my cheeks as I remembered special times on those banks. I thanked God for his goodness to me and to my family. I gazed again at the moving water as it rippled across the collection of rocks. I listened again to its babble. I drank in the moment. I walked away more certain than ever of this one thing: where Living Water flows life is still transformed and this is exactly where I want to be.

## *The Leader's Prayer:*

Spirit of God who moved over the face of the waters . . . lead me not only beside still waters, but lead me to places where Living Water flows. Lead me to banks of life where your water babbles and echoes and ripples with transforming power. Together, as leaders in your church, freshen us, persuade us, and ready us for all the challenges that stretch out before us. Keep us near streams of your wisdom and your Word so that we might draw strength from *this* water and be restored to ministry day by day. In the name of the One who is Living Water, even Jesus the Christ . . . Amen.

Breinigsville, PA USA
25 January 2010
231343BV00001B/2/P

9 781438 939223